W9-DJC-031

# Cacti and Other Succulents

# Cacti and Other Succulents

by Jack Kramer

Photographs by Don Worth

*Drawings by Robert Johnson*

Harry N. Abrams, Inc., Publishers, New York

## Author's Note

The photographs for this book were taken over a period of twenty years; from thousands of pictures, some two hundred were selected for this volume. The photographer, Mr. Don Worth, is an experienced gardener who grows over two hundred cacti and succulents.

If your favorite plant is missing, it was a question of space rather than preference on our part. We have tried to include both popular plants and some collector's items to acquaint you with the world of cacti and succulents.

Editor: Joanne Greenspun
Book design: Gilda Kuhlman

**Library of Congress Cataloging in Publication Data**

Kramer, Jack, 1927-
    Cacti and other succulents.

    Bibliography: p.
    Includes index.          Don Worth
    1. Cactus. 2. Succulent plants. I. Title.
SB438.K69      635.9′55      77-5881
ISBN 0-8109-2096-4

Library of Congress Catalogue Card Number: 77-5881

Published in 1977 by Harry N. Abrams, Incorporated, New York
All rights reserved. No part of the contents of this book may be reproduced without the written permission of the publishers

Printed and bound in Japan

# Contents

# Cacti and Other Succulents

# Introduction ✳ Plants For Everyone

If you are growing plants indoors, there is a good chance you have some succulent types, but may not know it. Unlike cacti, succulents are not easily recognizable and appear in many plant groups. The popular Crown of Thorns *(Euphorbia milii splendens)* is considered a succulent, as is the Wax Plant *(Hoya carnosa)*.

Cacti are recognizable by their unique shapes and spines, nature working at her best to equip plants to survive in their respective environments, but the cacti family is only one member of the thirty or more plant families which have succulent members. It is the largest family, and while all cacti are succulents, not all succulents are cacti.

Because of their ability to withstand dryness and untoward conditions—tempered by milleniums of time—succulent plants are prime candidates for indoor growing and are popular with people who want beautiful plants indoors but may not have time to care for them properly.

It is almost impossible to kill succulents; they have an intense desire to survive.

Cacti and succulents have been favorite houseplants for many years; it is only recently, however, that more species have become available for indoor growing. This book offers complete information on how to buy these plants, care for them, repot them properly, as well as how to use cacti and succulents for indoor decoration at windows or as floor plants. There are also special chapters on propagation, greenhouse growing, and a comprehensive discussion of cacti and succulents in landscape use. Finally, there is a chapter on very special species and varieties.

In addition to instructions on how to grow cacti and succulents, we have included nearly two hundred breathtaking photos in both color and black and white. To complete the picture we offer many helpful lists and drawings so you can grow these plants indoors and enjoy them fully all year long.

# One ✳ How Cacti and Succulents Grow

What could be more enjoyable than bringing color and cheer into your home with some of nature's most beautiful handiwork? Cacti and succulents possess the most varied shapes and leaves, colors and designs, patterns and growth habits in the plant world, and once you have become acquainted with these beauties you will want to grow them. A simple understanding of where these plants come from and what their basic shapes and flower forms are is the backbone of growing them. And because plant names are so important—knowing the botanical name is the only way to get the plant you really want—you must know a bit about plant families, species, and varieties.

## Why Cacti and Succulents Are Popular

Cacti and succulents are good indoor plants because they can, if necessary, adapt to adverse conditions like underwatering for many weeks, since nature has provided these plants with built-in "storage tanks." And most cacti and succulents are small- to medium-sized plants, just right for tiny apartments, windows, and confined spaces.

The variety of plants within the cacti and succulent group is incredible. Only the family Orchidaceae can offer an equally vast choice of beautiful plants. Many of the succulents, such as Echeverias and *Dudleya pulverulenta,* have exquisite foliage which is either chalk white or lined with red edges. The textured beauty of succulents like Haworthias and Gasterias makes them a desirable plant group for people seeking distinctive foliage plants. Other succulents like *Crassula argentea,* the Jade Plant, have a compact habit and ability to withstand adverse conditions; still other succulents, like *Kalanchoe blossfeldiana* (a popular Christmas plant) and *Hoya carnosa* (the old-fashioned Wax Plant), have striking red flowers and clusters of fragrant, waxy white flowers, respectively.

Cacti offer an equal assortment of handsome plants valued either for their shape or their flowers. For example, the Golden Barrel Cactus *(Echinocactus grusonii)* is a splendid sight; the lovely flowers of Zygocactus hybrids (Christmas cacti) decorate many homes during the holidays; and small cacti like the many colorful Rebutias are crowned with bright red flowers in fall. Small dish gardens of cacti can complement a windowsill; larger cacti, such as those of the Cereus group, are handsome room additions because they act as structural forms in the design of the room. Many cacti look like sculpture when placed against a wall; smaller cacti like Lobivias and Parodias indoors bear two- to four-inch flowers of extremely bright color.

## Where Plants Come From

Most but not all succulents are native to deserts. Those that are not adorn trees in rain forests, grow on mountainsides or near the sea, or thrive in the semiarid regions of North and South America, Africa, and Asia. Most cacti come from Mexico, but some grow in the Western deserts of the United States and high in the Cordilleras of Peru, Bolivia, and Argentina. Cacti such as Christmas Cactus and Rhipsalis inhabit the rain forests of Central America, and a few cacti even grow under the snow in British Columbia.

## Plant Shapes

If you are tired of the leafy sameness of foliage plants, succulents and cacti offer unequaled dramatic forms and unusual shapes that will add exciting contrast to your houseplants. For example, Euphorbias have contorted, bizarre shapes; Echeverias have rosettes of leaves that look like they have been carved from stone; and *Agave victoriae-reginae* has triangular, deep green leaves dramatically outlined in white, appearing like a huge tufted flower. Cacti can be columnar, like the magnificent organ pipe and candelabra cacti; barrel-shaped; star-shaped; or cascading, like Easter cacti. And the Old Man Cactus *(Cephalocereus senilis),* covered with white hair, resembles a puppet.

## Flowers

Cacti flowers are called silk flowers because in bloom they look like bright fabric. This symphony of color can add great beauty to the home. The fiery red flowers of the Rebutias, for example, are highly prized.

Unfortunately, most flowers last only a few days, but a healthy plant bears several flowers in succession, so bloom can continue for a week or more. Most cacti flowers are large for the size of the plant. Parodias and Lobivias have two-inch flowers on plants that are sometimes only a few inches in diameter.

Colorful flowers are well represented in the following cacti. Most of the plants listed are of small size, the majority being only two to four inches across. The exceptions to this are the Epiphyllums; these are sprawling plants that can take up space.

*Chamaecereus sylvestri* (Peanut Cactus). Dozens of blazing red blooms.
*Echinocactus horizonthalonius.* Frilly pink flowers.

*Echinocereus engelmannii.* Dramatic red-purple flowers.
*E. pectinatus rigidissimus.* A rainbow of colorful spines; pink flowers.
*E. triglochidiatus.* Fine pink to cerise flowers.
Echinopsis hybrids. White or pink flowers on tall stems; mainly night-blooming; lovely.
Epiphyllum hybrids. Large, striking flowers in an array of different colors.
*Lobivia aurea.* Two- to four-inch yellow flowers.
*L. backebergii.* Dazzling carmine blooms.
*L. callianthus.* Unusual, many-petaled pink flowers.
Lobiviopsis 'Stars and Stripes.' Delicate pink pointed petals; a real winner.
*Mammillaria bocasana* (Snowball or Powder Puff Cactus). Bright yellow flowers.
*M. fasciculata.* Small plant, but many pink flowers edged in white.
*M. hahniana* (Old Lady Cactus). Pink to reddish blooms.
*M. swinglei.* Delicate pink flowers edged in white.
*Notocactus leninghausii* (Golden Ball Cactus). Lemon yellow flowers on short stems.
*N. ottonis* (Indian Head). Bright yellow flowers.
*N. rutilans.* Blush white flowers; delightful.
*Parodia aureispina* (Tom Thumb Cactus). Small plant, but large yellow flowers.
*P. camarguensis.* Bright orange-red flowers; stunning.
*P. microthele.* A fine yellow-flowering gem.
*P. sanguiniflora* (Crimson Parodia). Best of the reds.
*Rebutia canigueralii.* Bright red flowers tinged yellow in the center.
*R. kupperana.* Free blooming, with many red flowers.
*R. minuscula* (Crown or Red Crown Cactus). Fine small red flowers.
*Trichocereus andalgalensis.* Large orange-red flowers; exquisite.
*T. auricolor.* Fiery orange blooms; spectacular.

As a rule, succulents do not have such startling flowers; most, such as Agaves and Aloes, bear small-to-medium blooms. But some succulents, like the Wax Plant *(Hoya carnosa),* with its white waxy blooms, and the Poinsettia *(Euphorbia pulcherrima),* with red bracts, are known for their color. (The latter, however, is not technically considered a true succulent.) Basically, succulents are grown for their colorful foliage and unusual shapes.

Succulent plants are somewhat larger in size

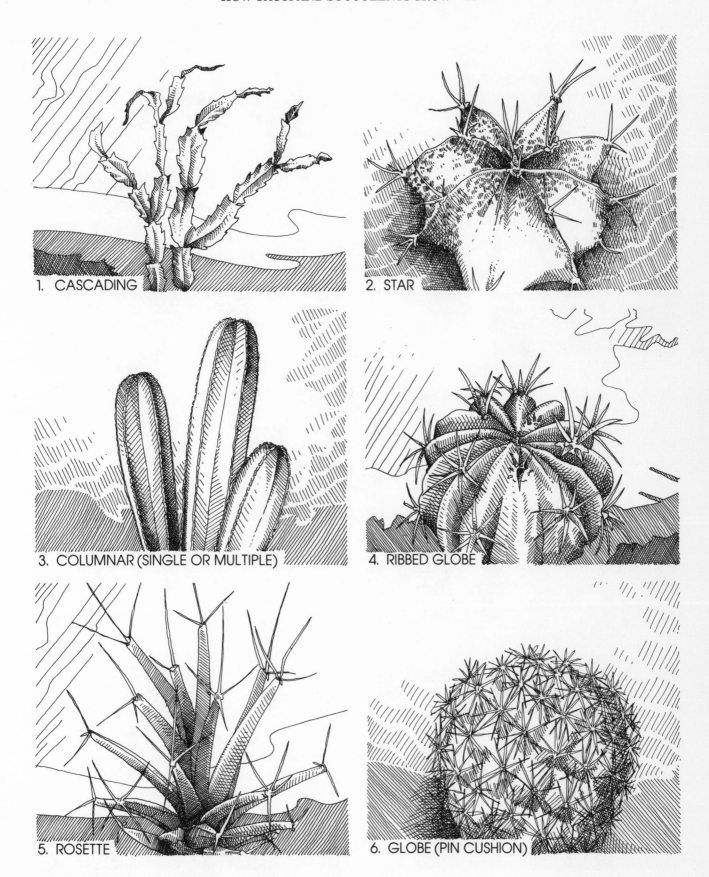

1. CASCADING

2. STAR

3. COLUMNAR (SINGLE OR MULTIPLE)

4. RIBBED GLOBE

5. ROSETTE

6. GLOBE (PIN CUSHION)

# SHAPES OF CACTI

1.  TOP (MULTIPLE OR SINGLE)

2.  SIDE

3.  BOTTOM

4.  SCALLOP (TERMINAL)

5.  SCALLOP (SIDE)

# FLOWER HABITS OF CACTI

than most cacti previously mentioned. Most of the plants in the following list are of medium size, up to sixteen inches.

Striking foliage are represented in these succulents:

*Aeonium arboreum* 'Schwarzkopf.' Greenish-black foliage.

*A. arboreum variegata.* Green leaves margined in cream color.

*A. canariense.* Large flattened rosettes of apple green leaves.

*Agave stricta.* Pointed leaves in a beautiful rosette.

*A. victoriae-reginae.* Narrow olive green leaves penciled white on the edges.

*Aloe brevifolia.* Clump growth; gray-green rosettes.

*A. striata* (Coral Aloe). Gray-green leaves bordered in red.

*Chirita sinensis.* Spectacular green leaves with yellow markings. From the Gesneriad family.

*Coleus aromatica.* Small bright apple green leaves serrated at edges.

*Cotyledon ladysmithiensis.* Apple green furry leaves.

*C. orbiculata.* Frosty leaves margined with red.

*C. undulata* (Silver Crown). Outstanding, with broad showy leaves beautifully waved at the margins.

*Crassula argentea* (Jade Plant). Bright green rubbery leaves.

*C. perforata* (String of Buttons). Alternating dark green leaves.

*Dudleya brittonii* (Chalk Lettuce). Broad leaves, startling white.

Echeveria. A large group; plants range in colors from shades of green to pale pink and purple.

E. 'Afterglow.' Chalk green leaves edged in white.

E. 'Big Curly.' Wavy-edged leaves; handsome.

E. 'Blondie.' Almost white in color.

*Euphorbia obesa* (Basketball Plant). Multicolored round globe; a beautiful oddity.

*Gasteria verrucosa* (Ox Tongue). Tapering pink and purple leaves.

*Graptopetalum filiferum.* An exquisite rosette of green leaves.

*Haworthia fasciata* (Zebra Haworthia). Dark green leaves banded with white dots.

*H. greenii.* Tufted brilliant green leaves.

*Hoya carnosa* 'Tricolor.' Yellow and green foliage.

*Kalanchoe beharensis* (Elephant Ears or Felt Plant). Large and floppy brown leaves.

*Kleinia repens.* Brilliant blue-green cylindrical leaves.

*Sedum morganianum* (Burro's Tail). Small beadlike apple green leaves.

*Senecio medley-woodii.* Looks as if it were carved from stone; apple green color.

## Plant Names

Some plants have common names—Crown of Thorns, Golden Barrel—but many do not. Common names are used frequently by hobbyists, but often a single plant may have several common names. Therefore, you should learn the Latin names so you are sure of getting the plant you want.

Cacti and succulents are arranged in groups; each group is called a genus. In each genus there are many members which are differentiated by taxonomists into species. Thus Echinocactus is a genus of many plants; *E. grusonii* is the species name. Species names are italicized, but genus names are not.

When a plant is hybridized (man-made pollinated) for better flower form or more compact growth, a variety name is given to the plant, such as 'Golden' or 'Pink Sunset.' Variety names follow species name in single quotes.

The source for botanical names in this book is *Hortus Third* (New York, 1976); however, in some cases I have opted for more common usage of catalogue and trade lists. These vary somewhat from standard botanical nomenclature. For example, the group Kleinia is referred to as both Kleinia and Senecio.

Taxonomists occasionally change plant names as new research is done; therefore, by the time this book goes to press, some botanical name changes are possible. In the plant lists throughout this book there is some duplication because some plants have many uses: for dish gardens, for windows, and so on.

*captions for plates 1–16:*

1. *Rebutia muscula (nivea)*
   Andes of South America

Many of the Rebutias prefer somewhat less sun than most other cacti. All are easily grown, and this species with one-inch flowers is no exception.

2. *Oscularia deltoides*
   South Africa

This shrubby succulent with triangular leaves forms an absolute carpet of blossoms in the spring. The blue-green foliage with reddish stems is attractive even when the plant is not in bloom.

3. Graptophytum 'Aphrodite'

This chalky-looking plant is a hybrid between *Graptopetalum paraguayense* and *Pachyphytum oviferum*. It is easily grown, and its trailing nature makes it ideal for wall pockets and hanging planters.

4. *Peperomia arifolia grandis*
   Brazil

Many of the Peperomias possess thick, shiny, hard-surfaced, and moisture-retentive leaves which distinctly place them within the succulent category. This particular plant is almost identical in appearance to *Peperomia sandersii*, the popular Watermelon Plant, but the foliage in this species is larger. It cannot stand constantly moist soil. Propagation is possible with single leaves.

5. Succulent Garden

This large garden creates a sensational impression during the winter months, when many Aloes are in bloom. Although located near sea level, in Hawaii, plants from widely varying conditions thrive here with the loving care that they are given.

6. Epiphyllum 'Conway's Giant'

The large, seven-inch blossoms of this Orchid Cactus are produced in May or June each year. This is a spineless cactus that grows best in a hanging basket with a light soil mixture. It prefers partial shade.

7. Succulents
   Lava flow, Mexico

Creating a natural rock garden, *Agave horrida* and *Sedum frutescens* find little soil in this black lava flow at an approximate seven-thousand-foot elevation north of Cuernavaca.

8. *Gymnocalycium anisitsii* X *G. mihanovichii*

Gymnocalycium species are such attractive plants as they exist in nature that few hybridizers have felt it necessary to work with them. However, this unnamed hybrid appears to possess many desirable qualities, including increased vigor.

9. *Echinocereus triglochidiatus*
   Southwestern United States

This is a winter-hardy species that produces a large quantity of flowers in spring and early summer. It is an easily grown plant, but requires full sun and generous root space.

10. *Mammillaria guelzowiana*
    Mexico

This popular Mammillaria produces one of the largest flowers in the genus. The blossom is more than two inches in diameter, and its deep purple-red color creates a jewel-like effect in its setting of white hair and red-brown, hooked spines. The plant is easy to grow, and it offsets very freely.

11. *Schlumbergera bridgesii*
    Bolivia?

Much confusion exists as to the correct name for the common Christmas Cactus. It has been known variously as *Zygocactus truncatus, Epiphyllum truncatus, Schlumbergera russelliana, Schlumbergera truncata,* and, more recently, *Schlumbergera* X *buckleyi*. At least two different species and many hybrids are involved in the complicated background of this plant, but it does not alter the fact that this epiphytic cactus remains one of the most satisfying succulents. It is ideal for hanging baskets, but must have the cooler, shortened days of winter in order to produce flowers.

12. *Lophocereus schottii* 'Monstrosus'
    Arizona; Northern Mexico

The Whisker Cactus has no ribs or spines, but consists of a column of green knobs and bumps. It is a choice plant, which must have full sun for normal development.

13. *Aloe arborescens*
    South Africa

The Candelabra Aloe produces two-foot-long leaves with horny teeth and reaches heights of fifteen feet. The brilliant flowers are produced in the winter. Young specimens may be grown in pots, but bloom is not certain.

14. *Trichocereus andalgalensis*
    Argentina

The three-inch flowers of this vigorous species appear in June. It is native to high altitudes and is tolerant of several degrees of frost.

15. *Chirita sinensis*
    South China

This succulent is a member of the Gesneriad family, which includes the common African Violet and the florist's Gloxinia. This is a slow-growing plant which must not be overwatered. In time the rosette of thick, rigid, hairy leaves will reach a diameter of one foot or more.

16. Succulent Garden

Several types of Agaves and Aloes are planted along a sloping bank next to a garden path in California. Many of these specimens have withstood several degrees of frost. In colder climates all of the species seen here may be grown in pots and then moved outside during the summer.

1

2

4

5

6

7    8

9   10

11

12

13

15

# Two ✳ Starting a Collection

What are you going to grow? Which plants and for what purposes? Most true hobbyists collect specific plants, but you can buy plants you like for one characteristic or another: shape, form, flower color. To start a collection, decide whether you will use the plants for (1) color, (2) accent, or (3) because of their rarity. Also decide whether you want miniature (to six inches), medium (to twenty-four inches), large (to forty inches), or giant plants. There are different sizes in each genus.

If you have a chance, visit a cactus and succulent nursery because what you select yourself will always be best. But if you cannot get to a nursery, at least send for mail-order catalogues, which have descriptions of plants and sometimes pictures. Or use this book as a guide to help you in your selection.

## Sources for Plants

Because of the expanding interest in plants, there are all sorts of places where you can buy cacti and succulents: nurseries and florist shops, five-and-tens, plant shops, mail-order suppliers, or plant departments of large stores. (Best of all, of course, would be to get free plants from friends' cuttings or divisions.) Because of the high price of plants, shop for the best for the least. Prices are *not the same* all over; I have seen identical Agaves for three dollars at one place and ten dollars at another place.

Besides price, what kind of plant you want

will determine where to get it. For instance, if you are seeking a rare species, the only source is mail order. On the other hand, the most popular cacti and succulents can be found in the other outlets.

Let us see what kinds of plants each source offers and what they charge.

1. Florists and nurseries generally have excellent quality plants, but usually their prices are quite high. You pay more because if a plant fails, most (but not all) of these sources will refund the cost or replace plants in a reasonable amount of time. Florists and nurseries carry the more popular species.

2. Plant shops and plant sections of department stores are not good places to buy cacti and succulents. These sources stock just a few species, nothing elaborate, or will not have specific or unusual types. Prices range from good to fair value; that is, the prices are lower than those at florists or nurseries but higher than at five-and-tens.

3. Five-and-tens have a better selection of cacti and succulents than most people think because they have carried these plants for decades. Prices are low, and although quality may not be superior, it is generally satisfactory. Five-and-tens carry about fifteen species, occasionally some rare ones.

4. Mail-order suppliers are by far the best source because they specialize in cacti and succulents. Prices are fair, and the quality is excellent since good stock is the suppliers' only business. Most mail-order suppliers publish

catalogues that list hundreds of plants. Do not worry about shipping: sophisticated packing methods make it possible to mail anywhere in the United States.

## How to Buy Plants

No matter where you purchase plants, always look for fresh, healthy ones. To determine if a plant is thriving, check the following:

1. The base of the plant—there should be no softness, bruises, or spots of any kind.

2. Leaves or bodies of plants—they should be firm and free of any bruises.

3. The soil—if it is caked, the plant has been in the pot a long time. Soil may be so caked that watering will be impossible. Touch the soil to feel how loose it is.

4. Overall color of the plant—if the body of the plant is pale in one area and dark in another, forget it because this denotes a possible virus at work. Color should be uniform, unless it is a variegated plant.

5. Obvious insects—mealybugs can be seen (they cluster near spines); aphids; red spider mites (tough to see); and scale (little black specklike pests).

6. Offsets (little plants at the base)—these are desirable since they are free plants which can be severed from the parent plant.

7. Name tags—name tags are important to determine what you have. If there is no name on the plant, ask for it to be put on a tag.

## When You Get Plants Home

No matter where you buy your plants, when you get them home they will need more care in the first few weeks than for the rest of their time with you. It takes plants at least two to three weeks to adjust to new conditions. Now is the time to give plants more attention than usual. Be sure the soil is evenly moist and the plants are doing well. If they seem to be suffering—that is, they look wan and the leaves are starting to brown off—move them to a new location.

Most newly bought plants should be put in a bright, but not sunny, temperate place for a few days. This is especially true for mail-order plants because they will have been in boxes for a time. But do not just set them in direct sun or the light may kill them. Condition the plants over a period of a week or so to direct sun: first put them in bright light, then in some sunlight, and finally into full sunlight.

When you get plants home, be sure there are no insects. Here is one foolproof way of finding out just what lurks within the soil: immerse the pots halfway in a sink of water for a few hours; any uninvited guests will appear on the surface of the soil. You should run this test with any plant because even the best nurseries occasionally have traveling pests.

Do not do any repotting for the first few weeks or you will shock the plants—adjusting to new conditions is shock enough. Even if the plants are in soilless mixes, let them be for some time. (See more about soilless mixes in Chapter 4.)

## Where to Put Plants

Plants need places just as people do, so position is everything. Fortunately, most cacti and succulents are small plants and can be accommodated in or near windows, where light is the best. A handsome arrangement is a window-shelving setup of plants. Buy shelves from suppliers, or make your own from glass or wood. Three shelves will hold over twenty-five plants in an average-sized window.

If you want flowers from your plants, you must put flowering plants like Parodias and Lobivias in east and south exposures; use other exposures for succulent foliage plants.

Here is a suggested window arrangement for a beginner's garden of cacti and succulents:

South and East windows:
  *Agave americana*
  *A. filifera*
  *Aloe aristata*
  *A. brevifolia*
  *Lobivia aurea*
  *Opuntia microdasys*
  *Parodia sanguiniflora*

West windows:
  *Crassula argentea*
  Echeveria hybrids
  *Euphorbia obesa*
  *E. splendens*
  *Gymnocalycium mihanovichii*
  *Hoya carnosa*

North windows:
  *Ceropegia woodii*
  *Gasteria maculata*

*Haworthia tessellata*
*Leuchtenbergia principis*
*Rebutia kupperana*
*Sansevieria hahnii*
*Stapelia variegata*
*Tradescantia fluminensis*

You might also want plants in other areas of the home. Kitchens and bathrooms are excellent spots for plants because hot running water creates humidity. A specimen treelike cacti or succulent makes a stunning accent in a living or dining room, and table plants (small ones like Gasterias and Haworthias) can be used for color in any room of the home, including the bedroom. And do not overlook hanging cacti and succulents for beauty in any area of the home.

## Size of Plants

Most cacti and succulents grow ever so slowly, so if you want a twelve-inch plant, do not buy a two-inch one and wait for it to grow; get one at least ten inches. Do not expect the fast growth of a Philodendron or a Begonia. Cacti and other succulents take years to mature, but they will provide color and beauty for many decades if properly cared for.

## The Best Plants to Buy

In most of my other houseplant books I have given an easy-to-grow list of various types of plants. Here, however, because cacti and succulents are generally amenable plants to grow (if given minimum culture), I did not include that list. Almost all varieties of cacti and succulents do well indoors. It is simply a matter of personal choice, a question of what you like.

As mentioned in Chapter 1, plants are classified into various genera, and each genera contains a number of different plants. Here is a basic list of genera to give you some idea of plants within each group.

### SUCCULENTS

**Adromischus.** Native to South Africa, these are mostly small plants with alternating leaves. Adromischus species make reliable indoor plants, grow slowly, and require no special care. The plants produce small, not overly attractive, flowers.

**Aeonium.** Shrubby plants with woody and branched stems; rosette growth of petal-like leaves. Spring-blooming flowers are pink, yellow, or red. Easy to grow in any light if given winter rest at 55°F; otherwise, grow plants in full sun. Use a rich sandy soil. Plants die after flowering but usually produce offsets. Best used as window or table plants.

**Agave.** Compact rosettes of very hard, generally pointed, fleshy leaves that grow close to the soil. Many species are beautifully marked. White flowers appear on a tall stem. Plants die after blooming, but since Agaves do not bloom for many years, this is of little importance. Propagate from the offsets at the base.

**Aloe.** These are either short-stemmed or tall shrublike plants with fleshy, horned or warted, pointed leaves fashioned into a rosette. Numerous red, yellow, or orange flowers appear on tall stems from February to September. Aloes are small, medium, or large plants. They defy abuse and still grow, making them excellent room plants.

**Bowiea.** Grown for its oddity rather than for its beauty. Produces a large spherical bulb, and in summer stringy-type stems with pale green leaves appear. Flowers are greenish-white. Grow in very sandy soil and keep the soil dry during winter.

**Ceropegia.** Usually cascading plants, with long stems and heart-shaped, colorful leaves. Small tubular flowers of various colors in the summer. Excellent as a room plant and can withstand neglect. Likes moisture in summer, dryness and rest (55°F) in winter.

**Cotyledon.** Shrubby plants with opposite or alternate rounded leaves that are sometimes covered with a whitish powder. Some Cotyledons are low growing and have pointed leaves; a few shed leaves every year; others have persistent leaves. Orange or red flowers. Cotyledons need a definite winter rest (55°F). Easily grown, these make handsome room plants.

**Crassula.** These succulent shrubs have opposite leaves, usually in a rosette shape. Some Crassulas have branching stems; others are low plants with dense foliage. Small white, yellow, or pink flowers in the summer. Generally easy-to-grow plants. Most popular is the Jade Plant, *C. argentea.*

**Dudleya.** These are beautiful rosette-shaped plants with white chalky leaves. Some species have finger-like leaves. Plants are either short-stemmed or grow close to the ground. Most Dudleyas are difficult as houseplants; they prefer the outside garden.

**Echeveria.** Beautiful succulents with fleshy

gray-green or green leaves that are often marked with deeper colors. Pink, red, or yellow bell-shaped flowers in clusters. Growth habit ranges from spreading clumps to small shrubs with stout stems. Many beautiful varieties. These make excellent room plants and require a somewhat dry winter rest at 55°F. Never get water on the leaves.

**Euphorbia.** This large genus has nine hundred species. Euphorbias have varied growth habits: many look like cacti; some are extremely dramatic in shape; and others are just odd. The flowers of most of these plants are brownish or greenish, except for the popular Crown of Thorns and the Christmas plant, Poinsettia. Most have spines on the leaves. Plants grow well in most situations; in fact, the dry atmosphere of most rooms suits them well. Plants like sun and an airy place and need little or very little water in winter, with somewhat cooler temperatures.

**Faucaria.** Very fleshy triangular leaves are held in angular rosettes; plants are generally stemless. Leaves are gray or green, tinged with red or spotted; toothed leaf margins. The daisy-like yellow or white flowers are large in proportion to the overall smallness of the plant.

**Gasteria.** These plants are related to the Aloes, but the leaves are often blunt and held in a fan shape, although some species grow in rosettes, especially as they age. The leaves are a dark green mottled with pale green or white; flowers are usually red and bell-shaped, with green tips, borne on slender stems. Very durable plants that tolerate shade and neglect.

**Haworthia.** Extremely variable in growth habit; some of the best-known ones resemble the smaller Aloes, but others make small towers of neatly stacked fleshy leaves or stemless rosettes. Leaf colors are also variable, from grayish through shades of green.

**Kalanchoe.** Native to tropical regions of America, Africa, and Southeast Asia, so plants cannot tolerate frost—they prefer moisture. Most species are branching, shrubby plants. Leaves may be smooth or felted; showy flowers in shades of red through yellow.

**Sansevieria.** Thick, patterned leaves grow in clusters and radiate up and out from the base; leaves range in shape from short, blunt triangles to long swords. These have been popular houseplants for generations, able to survive with the most casual care: dry air, little light, uneven temperatures, and infrequent watering.

**Sedum.** Some Sedums are tiny and trailing; others are bushy and upright. All have fleshy leaves, but size, shape, and color are highly variable among the species, and some are even deciduous. Flowers are usually small and starlike, in moderately large clusters.

**Sempervivum.** These stemless plants have tightly packed rosettes of leaves. Little offsets cluster around the parent rosette; the parent dies after flowering, leaving the offsets to form new clumps. Flowers are not showy. All species and varieties need sun, good drainage, and generous summer watering.

**Stapelia.** There are more than one hundred species of Stapelias; most have a dwarf habit and are branched at the base. The flowers are more bizarre than beautiful and generally have deep purple coloring with yellow markings inside the bloom. (Some have an unpleasant odor.) Grow the plants in shallow pots and be careful not to overwater them; in winter keep the soil just barely moist. Stapelias like some sun and respond best in moderate temperatures of 55 to 70°F.

## CACTI

**Astrophytum.** Sea Urchin Cactus, Bishop's Cap, and Goat's Horn Cactus are in this group. Usually globular-shaped or with prominent ribs; some have a covering of woolly hair. These small plants are excellent indoors. Flowers are yellow to red.

**Cephalocereus.** The familiar Old Man Cactus exemplifies this group: tall columnar or branching growth, usually covered by long woolly hair. Most flower at night, but only rarely indoors.

**Cereus.** Eventually these make tree-sized plants to thirty feet or more, but young ones are fine houseplants. Large (to eight inches) white flowers on old plants appear at night. Blue-green stems.

**Chamaecereus.** Bright red flowers. Small, clump-forming plants; short shoots branch from the base to produce the clump effect.

**Cleistocactus.** Some species outdoors grow to six feet. Recognizable by a definite narrowing of the stem near the growing point. Stems are generally columnar, often leaning, and so thickly covered with spines that the stem surface is hardly visible. These are easy to grow, with profuse orange to red flowers.

**Coryphantha.** These globular or cylindrical plants (some as much as twelve inches high) with interesting spine patterns have large yellow, red, or purple flowers. A definite winter rest is required.

**Echinocactus.** Includes the barrel cacti. These are heavily spined and produce flowers from near the crown of mature plants. Young plants are good container subjects; mature specimens may be several feet tall.

**Echinocereus.** Free-branching clusters or mounds of erect or prostrate stems, usually less than a foot tall. All have highly ornamental spines densely covering the plant surfaces. Long-lasting showy flowers (to four inches across).

**Echinopsis.** Small cylindrical or globular plants with definite vertical ribs. Long-tubed, many-petaled flowers in shades of white, yellow, pink, or red; flowers may reach six to eight inches in length. These are among the least particular cacti as to soil, amount of water, and light.

**Epiphyllum.** Spineless plants with large saucer-like flowers in many colors. Easy to grow, but need support. Provide filtered light and a well-drained sandy soil. Plants like to be rootbound.

**Gymnocalycium.** Plant bodies are usually globular, with regularly arranged protrusions that give them the name Chin Cactus. Red, pink, or white flowers; plants are less than ten inches tall.

**Lobivia.** Small two- to four-inch globular or cylindrical plants, with big and showy red, yellow, pink, orange, purple, or lilac flowers (flowers sometimes nearly as big as the plants).

**Mammillaria.** Small, cylindrical, or globe-shaped; may be single-stemmed or clustered. Small red, pink, yellow, or white flowers arranged in a circle near the plant's top.

**Notocactus.** These small ball cacti are easy to grow and are free-flowering. Yellow or purplish-red flowers.

**Parodia.** These small species are similar to Notocactus. They flower heavily, have decorative (usually curving) spines, and need little attention.

**Rebutia.** Small, globular species. Bear flowers from the sides or from around the base; flowers are large for the size of the plant.

**Rhipsalis.** Some of these trailing plants have flattened stems, but most have slender, cylindrical segments. Flowers are small and not showy.

**Schlumbergera.** One of the popular holiday-blooming cactus. Flowers can be white, cream, orange, red, or fuchsia. Need lots of sun in fall and winter.

**Zygocactus.** Another holiday-blooming cactus, these are forest dwellers, generally growing on trees. Flowers are borne on terminal shoots and are stunning, usually pink or red. The leaves are jointed, flattened green stems that have a tendency to cascade. Needs even moisture all year, good air circulation, and a six-week period of darkness in late fall to force flower buds.

17. *Crassula argentea (portulacea)*
    South Africa

The vigorous Jade Plant is one of the most popular succulents, and it is an ideal pot plant. It is slow growing, but becomes a shrub five to ten feet tall when grown in the open ground in subtropical climates, where it withstands a few degrees of frost. Although grown principally for its thick, shiny leaves and its bonsai appearance, it may also produce small pink to red blossoms in the spring.

18. *Cephalocereus senilis*
    Mexico

The Old Man Cactus may grow to forty feet in its native habitat, but its slow growth and less than ideal conditions keep it much smaller than that in cultivation. For best appearance it requires full sun and a lowering of temperature in the winter in order to induce dormancy. The long white hair eventually loses its beautiful appearance on the lower part of the column, but it may be topped and rooted in order to produce another plant. The lower part of the plant will also produce new growth.

19. *Echeveria elegans*
    Mexico

Out of all the hundreds of species and hybrid Echeverias, this is probably the best known. It is vigorous and rapid growing, forming many offsets which eventually create a solid carpet. The beautiful translucent leaves are silver blue and appear to have been carved from some exotic form of alabaster. Pink and yellow flowers appear in the spring.

20. *Crassula barbata*
    Africa

The hairy, two-inch-diameter rosettes have a symmetrical arrangement of leaves in groups of four. Each plant dies upon producing its inflorescence of tiny white blossoms. However, just prior to this event, each rosette produces a large quantity of offsets from the base.

21. *Crassula tetragona*
    Africa

This is a vigorous, small, shrubby plant which is excellent for bonsai effects. Like many of the Crassulas it prefers somewhat cooler temperatures and slightly more water than many other African succulents. The arrangement of needle-like leaves in rows of four creates a perfect cross when viewed from above.

22. *Sedum morganianum*
    Mexico

The Burro's Tail is an extremely popular plant for hanging baskets and will tolerate an amazing amount of abuse, growing in both dry and wet climates that are frost-free. Perfect specimens are difficult to achieve, as the beautiful pale green leaves detach themselves at the slightest touch. Each leaf is capable of producing a new plant.

23. *Sedum oxypetalum*
    Mexico

This deciduous-type shrub, with peeling, papery bark, is an ideal subject for bonsai effects. It is rather slow growing and may remain in the same pot for years.

24. Kalanchoe 'Rose Leaf'

This hybrid of *Kalanchoe beharensis* and *Kalanchoe tomentosa* combines the best qualities of both plants, including vigor. The soft, velvety leaves range from green to gray to brown, depending upon the amount of light, water, and fertilizer provided.

25. *Kalanchoe daigremontiana*
    Madagascar

Like several other Kalanchoes, this easily grown succulent produces small plants on the edges of the leaves. It grows rapidly to become a specimen approximately two feet high.

26. *Kalanchoe beharensis*
    Madagascar

Large, brown, felted leaves, up to a foot long, are typical of this well-known plant. The heavy, folded leaves cluster at the top of a single knotted trunk, which may in time reach a height of eight or ten feet.

27. Echeveria 'Evening Star'

The large, folded leaves of *Echeveria dactylifera* and the soft, blue-violet shading of *Echeveria shaviana* are brought together in this large hybrid, which grows to a foot or more in diameter. Offsets occur at rare intervals, but the plant may also be propagated from bracts on the tall inflorescence or by topping the plant in order to force numerous sprouts.

28. *Pachyphytum viride*
    Mexico

The three-inch-long leaves of this plant assume a bronzy color in strong light during the winter. As with many other members of the Crassula family, additional plants may be secured through leaf propagation.

29. Bowl of Sempervivums
    Europe; Asia; North Africa

Hundreds of Hen and Chicks hybrids are in existence, and they are very valuable plants for rock gardens in cold climates. They tend to grow rapidly, and, forming many offsets, produce a beautiful carpet of multicolored rosettes. Once an individual plant produces its inflorescence of red-lavender flowers, it dies.

30. *Aeonium pseudotabulaeforme* (top)
    Canary Islands

    *Graptopetalum paraguayense* (bottom)
    Mexico

This sprawling, dark green Aeonium and the trailing, light gray Graptopetalum form a satisfying combination for a hanging basket. The Graptopetalum, commonly known as Ghost Plant, is readily propagated from the easily detached leaves.

31. *Pachyphytum oviferum*
    Mexico

A heavy coating of white powder covers the one and one-half inch leaves of this plant. Like the bloom on grapes, the powdery coating is easily marred. Each leaf, when propagated, will provide an additional plant.

32. *Echeveria linguaefolia* (top)
    Mexico

    Graptophytum 'Aphrodite' (bottom)

This species of Echeveria is atypical and bears a strong resemblance to some of the Sedums and Pachyphytums. The lower plant is a bigeneric hybrid between *Graptopetalum paraguayense* and *Pachyphytum oviferum*. Both specimens, having a trailing tendency, are happy growing in a wall pocket.

33. Echeveria 'Blondie'

Pale yellowish-green leaves with slight crenulation form a foot-wide rosette which hides the pot it is growing in. Like most Echeverias, this plant is grown for its foliage rather than for the flowers, which tend to be insignificant.

34. *Sedum hintonii*
   Mexico

This low-growing, cushion-forming plant is prized for its pale blue-green leaves, which are heavily covered with hair. It is a warmth-loving succulent which tends to rot with overwatering during winter dormancy.

35. Echeveria 'Doris Taylor'

This vigorous hybrid between *Echeveria pulvinata* and *Echeveria setosa* is one of the most popular in this genus. The beautiful hairy rosettes, up to eight inches in diameter, produce rather large orange-red flowers. Offsets are the common means of propagation.

36. *Cotyledon ladysmithiensis*
   Cape Province

This is a dwarf, freely branching shrub that may grow to eight inches in height. It is easily grown and is one of the most satisfying succulents.

37. *Echeveria subrigida*
   Mexico

This spectacular plant with heavy, powdery white leaves will always be somewhat uncommon since it never produces offsets. It grows to a foot in diameter, and the leaves assume a red cast on the edges in bright sun. The orange and red flowers are unusually large for this genus. Perfect specimens are rare as the powdery coating is easily marred.

38. *Sempervivum ciliatum rubrum*
   Bulgaria; Macedonia

The dark cherry red color of this Sempervivum is a beautiful foil for the hairiness of the leaves. The two-inch plants, like most Sempervivums, come from mountainous areas and are winter hardy in cold climates.

39. *Sempervivum soboliferum*
   Northern Europe; Asia

The two-inch rosettes of this plant produce many ball-shaped offsets which detach themselves at the slightest touch. Rolling down the steep slopes where the plants normally grow, they then form new colonies wherever they lodge.

40. *Dudleya brittonii*
   Baja, California

Of all the powdery-leafed succulents, this is one of the most desirable. The white rosette may reach a foot or more in diameter but, unfortunately, never produces offsets. Propagation is by seed. Perfect specimens are extremely rare, as even an insect crawling over the leaves may mar the coating of powder.

41. *Aloe plicatilis*
   Cape Province

This slow-growing Fan Aloe eventually forms a bush or small tree to fifteen feet high. It is well adapted to pot cultivation and produces scarlet flowers.

42. *Aeonium urbicum*
   Canary Islands

Many hybrids within the Aeonium genus have appeared naturally in the subtropical gardens of California and the Mediterranean countries. Exact identification is almost as difficult as it is within the Sempervivum genus, where the same problem exists. The plant in this photograph produces a foot-wide rosette of shiny, light green leaves atop a single trunk which sometimes branches at the base. It is a vigorous, fast-growing succulent, but cannot withstand freezing temperatures.

43. *Aloe polyphylla*
   South Africa

One of the less-common succulents, the Spiral Aloe, named for the spiral arrangement of the leaves in older plants, is a spectacular specimen with translucent, pale green leaves and may reach two feet or more in diameter. It almost never offsets, but sometimes older plants may divide. Propagation is by seed, which is scarce. Despite the somewhat delicate appearance of its leaves, it is native to eight-thousand-foot altitudes, where light snow may occur briefly during the winter. It likes moist soil and moderate to cool summer temperatures.

44. *Aeonium spathulatum*
   Canary Islands

This small, shrubby species produces rosettes two to three inches in diameter, and it likes moist air and generous watering, especially during the winter growing period. Yellow flowers appear in the spring.

45. *Aloe variegata*
   Cape Province

The Partridge Breast or Tiger Aloe is perhaps the most widely grown Aloe for windowsill cultivation. It grows to one foot in height, producing numerous offsets and red blossoms in late winter or early spring.

46. *Beaucarnea recurvata*
   Southeast Mexico

The Pony Tail Plant or Elephant's Foot forms an enormous swollen base which rests on top of the soil. The luxuriant tuft of three-foot-long leaves in this specimen almost hides the interesting trunk. Indoors it grows in a warm south window, needing a pedestal to accommodate the long leaves. Growing in open ground in subtropical areas, the plant may reach a height of twenty feet, with multiple crowns.

47. *Faucaria tigrina*
   Cape Province

The Tiger's Jaws is one of the more vigorous members of the Mesembryanthemum family. It grows rapidly, producing many offsets, and the two- to four-inch plants eventually form a solid mass. The flowers are golden yellow.

48. *Peperomia rauhii*
   Peru

This new species is one of the many succulent Peperomias which are well suited to pot culture. The thick green leaves are one inch long.

49. *Monadenium guentheri*
   Kenya

This member of the Euphorbia family loses most of its tiny, stemless leaves during the resting period. It grows to eight inches high and is a good pot plant.

50. *Portulacaria afra*
   South Africa

The Elephant Bush is an admirable succulent for growing as a bonsai in a small pot. The untrained specimen shown here has reached a height of four feet. Some varieties have beautifully variegated foliage. All types are easily grown.

51. *Bursera microphylla*
   Southwest United States; Northern Mexico

The Elephant Trunk Tree is a natural bonsai from desert regions and is well adapted to pot culture. In its native habitat it grows to more than thirty feet.

52. *Huernia pillansii*
   South Africa

This succulent produces numerous two- to three-inch-tall, soft-bristled stems from a common root. The exotic star-shaped, rust red flowers appear in groups of two or three at the base of the young stems. The plant is sensitive to over-watering.

53. *Lithops lesliei*
   South Africa

The well-known Living Stone Plants are slow growing, but a well-maintained pot of them provides a beautiful example of nature's art of camouflage. They are less than two inches tall, and their blossoms almost hide the plants. They must be watered with utmost restraint during the winter resting period.

54. *Haworthia truncata*
   South Africa

One of the most unique plants is this succulent with leaves which look as if they had been chopped off. The truncated ends are translucent and filter the intense light of its native habitat. It is extremely slow growing and must be watered cautiously. Like most Haworthias, it prefers partial shade in cultivation.

55. Aeonium 'Ballerina'

Innumerable hybrids exist among the Aeoniums, but this is one of the most unique. The slightly sticky leaves, edged in white, produce beautiful rosettes four or five inches in diameter on a small, shrubby plant.

56. *Euphorbia obesa*
   Cape Province

The Basketball Plant is one of the most common Euphorbias for pot culture, as it is extremely durable and remains under five inches in diameter. The insignificant male and female flowers are borne on separate plants, and propagation is by seed only.

57. *Euphorbia ingens*
   South Africa

This is one of the larger members of the Euphorbia genus, becoming a spiny, succulent tree twenty-five to thirty feet tall. However, it may also be retained as a relatively small pot plant. The specimen seen here is fifteen to eighteen feet tall, growing in a warm, frost-free climate.

58. Echeveria 'Big Curly'

The large cabbage-leaf type of Echeveria generally prefers more warmth than the smaller, plain-leafed type. This plant may grow to eighteen inches in diameter, with reddish-tinged leaves in bright sun. The tall inflorescence of orange-red flowers is produced in autumn. Offsets occur sparingly, but the plant may also be topped and rooted in order to force the old trunk to produce sprouts.

59. *Senecio medley-woodii*
   Natal

This beautifully grown greenhouse specimen, with gray, felted leaves, was grown in bright sun, with caution in watering, in order to achieve such a remarkable effect. It is a very slow-growing succulent and should be pinched in order to produce a branching plant.

60. *Argyroderma testiculare*
   Cape Province

This stemless, extremely succulent plant commonly possesses only two leaves, which are smoothly sculptured and tend to resemble white marble. It is a tiny species, less than two inches high, and it must be watered cautiously during the winter resting period.

61. *Anacampseros alstonii*
   South Africa

The different species of the Anacampseros genus vary widely in appearance. This particular one forms a turnip-like caudex on top of the soil from which as many as three hundred branches may sprout. It is a small plant with white flowers less than one inch across.

62. *Lampranthus spectabilis*
   Cape Province

Of all the Ice Plants, this sprawling succulent is one of the most widely grown. It is a common ground cover in subtropical climates such as California and the Riviera, and in the spring it provides a solid carpet of red-purple blossoms two to three inches in diameter. It may also be grown in containers.

17

18

19    20

21          22              23

24    25

26

27

28

29

30

31

32

33

34

35

36

38

39

40

41

42    43

44

45

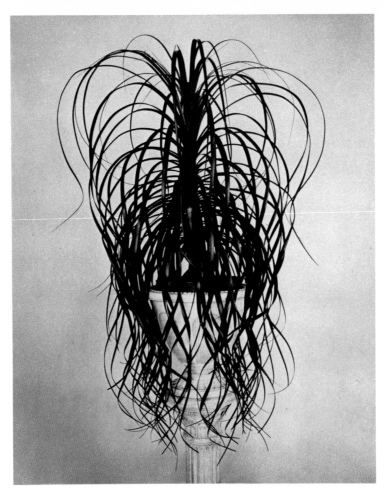

46

47

49   50

51

52

53

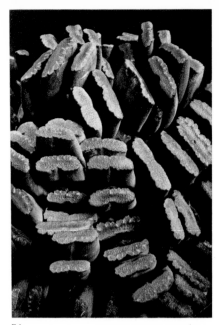

54

55

56

57

59

60

61

62

# Three ❋ Growing Cacti and Succulents

The proper cultivation of all plants involves careful attention to water, light, humidity, air circulation, feeding, and pest and disease control. However, each group of plants—orchids, Gesneriads, cacti, succulents, for example—has its own cultivation idiosyncrasies. There are certain do's and don'ts for each group, but as you grow plants you will gain this expertise. What follows is an overall discussion of the do's and don'ts for succulents and cacti; specific recommendations appear in the plant descriptions in other parts of this book.

## Light

Succulents and cacti need all the light they can get to grow into beautiful specimens, although when in a shaded situation, such as a dark corner, plants will survive; they just will not grow. And if you want flowers, the plants definitely must have some sun during the day. I had a few cacti in bad light and inadequate humidity. The plants did not die (in fact, they are still green accents), but they certainly have not grown and prospered. So for plants' maximum health, put them near windows. In spring, fall, and winter, succulents and cacti can take as much direct sun as possible. But in summer the plants should be shielded from the strong, direct sun rays. Use curtains, venetian blinds, or roll-ups.

Light at an east or south window is the best because it is bright and provides a few hours of sun. At west exposures plants get intense after-noon sun, which is fine for only some plants. North exposures are always a problem, but there are succulents and cacti that will grow, such as Wax Plants, Sansevieria, Christmas Cactus, and Rhipsalis. Put plants as close as possible to the window, but in winter move plants back so they will not get chilled.

Also consider reflected light; for example, plants on bookshelves painted white will receive a fair amount of light. Always face plants that are away from windows to the light. Light in the center of a room is generally poor, so if you must grow plants there, occasionally move them to window areas so they can gain their strength.

## Temperature and Ventilation

Average fall, winter, and spring home temperatures, say 75°F by day and 65°F at night, suit most succulents and cacti; the higher summer temperatures will not harm plants. Most cacti and succulents need a rest in the winter, so if home temperatures then drop to 65°F and 55°F, plants will benefit, especially flowering plants (a good winter chill helps promote flower buds). But *never* let winter home temperatures drop below 55°F in the growing area.

Plants must have good ventilation; rarely do any plants grow in stagnant areas. Your plants need a buoyant atmosphere, which means air circulation in the growing area. A good circulation of air thwarts fungus diseases, which proliferate in stagnant conditions, and contributes to the overall health of your plants. Most of the year leave a window open slightly, being careful not to let your cacti and succulents sit in a direct draft from windows, heating units, or cooling ducts. Drafts can almost kill cacti and succulents. In winter, keep a small fan on at low speed to help air circulate if you cannot leave windows open.

## Watering and Feeding

In nature cacti and succulents are drought-resistant plants because they can store water. But remember that home conditions for container plants are quite unlike those outside. For one thing, roots cannot stretch far for moisture, so plants have a tougher time growing. Thus the proper watering of your cacti and succulents is vital. Most people either water their houseplants too much or too little, but succulent and cactus plants can adjust either way, as long as they get *some* water.

But why make them adjust? Why not establish a definite schedule so your indoor plants will do their best? To set up a schedule, first consider the size of the container. Plants in small containers—three to four inches—need more frequent watering than plants in ten-inch pots because the soil in small pots dries out faster. A second consideration is the material of which the container is made: soil in clay pots dries out quicker than soil in plastic or glazed containers. Also consider light and temperature conditions: do not water on cool, cloudy days because there will not be enough light and without light, plants cannot assimilate water. And in spring and summer, when temperatures are high, plants need more water than in fall or winter because of evaporation.

A good watering schedule is to water plants once a week in early spring, twice a week in full spring, and three times a week in summer, which is when plants are in active growth. In fall, start tapering off water to twice a week, then once a week, to only occasional watering in winter—besides a rest from high temperatures, as we said, plants need a rest from watering. If you do water too much in the winter, your plants will bear abnormal growth, be susceptible to rot, and not bloom in summer. (Exceptions are Christmas and Easter cacti and hybrids, and Epiphyllums, which have leaflike stems and need winter watering.) Plants will give you hints as to when to resume your watering schedule: new growth and a perkier appearance. So adjust your watering schedule to the seasons;

your plants will excel.

However, no matter what kind of watering schedule you adopt, water properly. This means saturating the soil and then letting it dry out. Scanty waterings every few days will harm plants because only pockets of soil will get wet rather than all of it. Some roots will reach these pockets, but others will not, and they will, of course, die off. Water until excess water pours out of the drainage holes. Remove excess water from drip trays or saucers—do not let your cacti and succulents stand overnight in water.

Tepid tap water is fine for your plants, but icy cold water can shock them. Try to water in the morning rather than at night because water is not absorbed as readily as it is during the day, when there is light.

*Never* spray succulents and cacti with water or let water drip on plants. If you do, fungus diseases may hit the plants. I lost one of my prize Golden Barrel Cacti because water was dripping on its crown from a plant above. My plant was dead in three days: the crown completely rotted out. Every month or so take the plants to the sink and immerse them in water to the pot rim for about twenty minutes. This soaking helps leach out any toxic salts that may accumulate from overfeeding, and it refreshes plants.

Overfeeding can kill succulents and cacti because these slow-growing plants cannot absorb too much food—overfeeding will force them to grow at an unnatural rate. This forced growth will literally burn out a plant's energy. Plants in small pots really need no feedings; fish emulsion about once a month while plants are growing (but not at all the rest of the year) is fine if you want to give small plants something. Plants in pots larger than ten inches will, after a year, need some feeding; use a ten-ten-five food (ten percent nitrogen, ten percent phosphorus, five percent potassium) every other watering in spring and summer only. And remember these five feeding rules: (1) Never feed sick plants; (2) never feed plants in winter; (3) never give excessive doses of food; (4) never feed newly potted plants; and (5) never feed very young plants.

## Pest Control

Most houseplants eventually get attacked by various insects, but succulents and cacti rarely do because the plants are tough, preventing insects from piercing them. But if you do not take proper care of your succulents and cacti, or if you introduce pests via other houseplants, insects just might strike.

If you are not properly cultivating your plants, foliage will turn yellow, green stems will turn brown, or there may be abnormal growth or none at all. The chart below summarizes poor culture conditions.

If all your conditions are good—that is, plants do not exhibit any of the chart symptoms—but something is still wrong with your cacti and succulents, look for insects. Insects hide, so look carefully at stem axils, undersides of leaves, and any hidden plant parts not visible at first glance. Lift the pot so you can really see the undersides of leaves; tilt it further to allow you to see every part of the plant. You are looking for very small insects like mealybugs and scale (other plant bugs are large enough to be seen easily). If necessary, use a small magnifying glass.

Once you find insects, you have to know what they are before you try to eliminate them; know what you are fighting before you do battle. Study the following descriptions of the common house-plant insects, and then note the preventatives necessary to kill the specific pests.

*Aphids* are the most common pests to infest cacti and succulents. These small, green to black, soft-bodied creatures eat growing shoots and flower parts, thus distorting the young growth. To control aphids, use nicotine sulfate or malathion; be sure to water plants the day before you apply the preparation and keep plants shaded for a few hours after you apply preventatives.

*Mealybugs* cause extensive plant damage once they establish themselves on a plant. These fuzzy, cottony, gray or white insects lurk on spines, stems, and roots. Carefully spray plants with a solution of nicotine sulfate or malathion to kill mealybugs, or dip cotton swabs in alcohol and then dab the bugs.

| SYMPTOM | PROBABLE CAUSE | REMEDY |
| --- | --- | --- |
| No new growth | Too much water; soil is compacted; roots are decayed | Repot in fresh soil mixture (see Chapter 4); adjust watering practices |
| Yellow stems or leaves | Plant is too dry and gets too much heat | Provide better ventilation and more moisture in the air |
| Stems or leaves turn yellow | Iron deficiency from soil being too alkaline | Test pH of soil; add iron chelates if reaction is neutral to alkaline |
| Pale color on new growth | Root injury | Trim away dead or damaged roots; repot plant |
| Elongated growth | Not enough light | Move plant to location with more light |
| Failure to bloom, or very few flowers | Too much nitrogen, no winter rest, or both | Use fertilizer low in nitrogen, higher in phosphorus; give plants winter rest |
| Flower buds drop | Temperature is low or too fluctuating; plant is in draft | Move plant to warmer, draft-free location |
| Soft or mushy growth | Too much moisture; temperature too low | Reduce moisture, cut away soft parts, and dust cuts with Captan |
| Corky skin on stems | A natural development on some cacti as they age | |
| Plant has glassy, translucent look beginning in fall or winter | Frost damage | No cure; to prevent, keep plant dry, be sure it is not subjected to too low temperatures |

*Root-knot nematode* is a microscopic round-worm that penetrates plant roots, rotting them and causing swellings that look like beads on a string. Plants become stunted and pale. Sometimes an infected plant can be saved by trimming the roots and repotting the plant.

*Scale* is the most stubborn pest to kill. Scale look like brown spots about the size of a pinhead; they have a hard-shell covering. If the infestation is mild, pick off scale with a toothpick. Or mix steeped tobacco with laundry soap in a bucket of water. Use malathion for heavy attacks.

*Thrips and red spiders* look like small yellow or white spots on plant leaves or stems. Use nicotine sulfate or malathion.

*Ants* should be kept under control because they carry and thus help spread aphids from one plant to another. Use appropriate ant preventatives.

## Fungus Diseases

Fungus diseases are mainly caused by bad growing conditions, such as too much water, excessive moisture plus lack of light, and bruises and improperly healed cuts. Rot is probably the only disease that will bother your cacti and succulents. Rot, a blackish or brownish discoloration of leaves or stems, is caused by bacterial or fungal spores. If your plants get rot, cut away the rotted tissue; do a rather good surgical job and always cut more area than necessary to be sure the infection does not spread. After cutting, rub charcoal over the wound to help promote healing. Most rotting appears at the plant base if you are overwatering, so be sure drainage is excellent. Corky patches on cactus stems are quite natural, especially in large cacti.

# Four ✳ Repotting

Many garden books do not emphasize the repotting process (potting plants in fresh soil), yet repotting is necessary so plants can continue to receive vital nutrients from soil. When you consider repotting you must also decide what kind of soil and container you will use. And you must plan to groom your cacti and succulents to keep them at their peak. Finally, repotting is easy with most plants, but cacti especially are tricky because of their spines and hard-to-handle shapes. But if you learn the few tricks presented in this chapter, repotting your cacti and succulents will be as easy as repotting other houseplants.

## Soil Mixes

Many cacti and succulents are desert dwellers, but this does not mean that they should be potted in sand. They need a good soil mix. People used to mix their own soil by using equal parts of sand, soil, and leaf mold, but today soil mixes are sold in packages. There are hobby-sized packages that contain enough soil for just three or four six-inch containers to three-cubic-foot bags that will provide enough soil for several plants in very large containers. The larger bag is always the most economical; if you do not need all that soil immediately, store the excess in a cool, dry place in airtight containers. You can also buy bulk soil, which is the best because it is what the nursery uses. And of course you can see, feel, and smell this soil. Run your hand through it; it will feel mealy and porous, like a well-done baked potato. Smell it; it will have that woodsy, outdoor odor.

Packaged soils are sold under various trade names and in a variety of mixes, such as houseplant, African Violet, or cactus soil. To determine if a package contains a good soil—one that has all nutrients, is porous to air, and water can go through it—squeeze the bag: the package should feel crumbly.

I usually buy a packaged cactus soil mix and add two cups of sand. (If I have some houseplant soil on hand, I add some sand to it; you can buy sand in packages at nurseries.) I also add some charcoal chips to the cacti soil because they keep the soil sweet and increase its porosity. Do not use the man-made soilless mixes because they have few nutrients, and in these mixes plants must be fed every watering.

The potting medium called fir bark (used for potting orchids) is excellent for epiphytic (air-loving) succulents and cacti. Fir bark is also good for the jungle-type succulents and cacti, such as Christmas Cactus; add one cup of fir bark to a six-inch pot of standard cactus soil.

## Containers

There are so many types of containers—wooden, plastic, clay, ceramic, and brass—that making a selection is a problem and can cost money. The ordinary terra-cotta pots are ideal because water evaporates through their porous walls. In plastic or ceramic containers, which are not porous, the moisture stays in the soil; the walls have no air spaces, so evaporation is impossible.

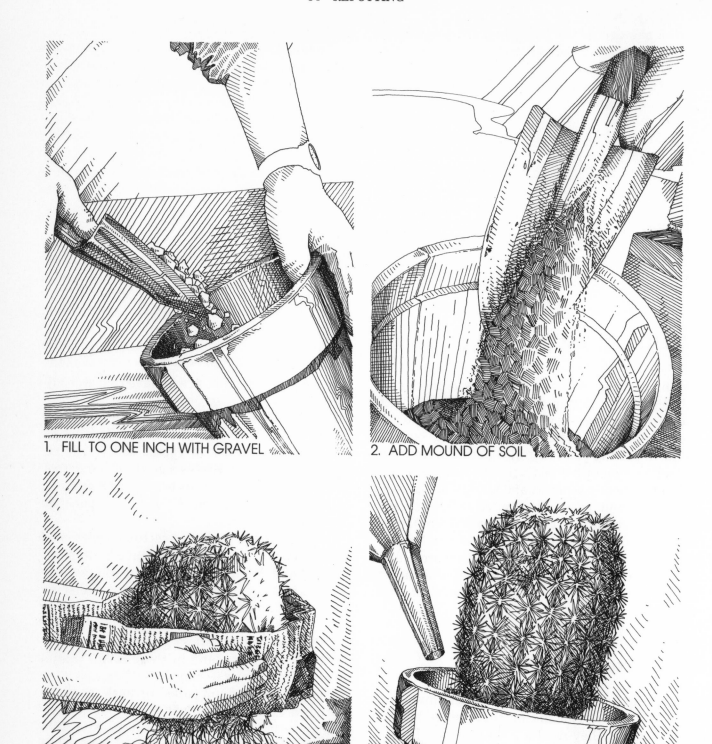

1. FILL TO ONE INCH WITH GRAVEL

2. ADD MOUND OF SOIL

3. HOLDING CACTUS WITH NEWSPAPER, INSERT IN POT

4. FILL IN SOIL USING A FUNNEL, PRESS SOIL WITH STICK

# POTTING A SMALL CACTUS

Also, the earth color of terra-cotta pots blends well with most interiors, and the pots are relatively inexpensive.

Terra-cotta pots come in sizes ranging from three to twenty-four inches in diameter and in three heights: shallow, medium, and tall. The shallow and medium heights are the best for most succulents and cacti.

Many ceramic pots have no drainage holes, so watering plants can be tricky. A good solution is to plant in a terra-cotta pot and then put the clay pot inside the ceramic one. Wooden planter bins, tubs, and boxes are quite satisfactory and often complement indoor interiors.

## The Process

Your succulents and cacti will be small, in four-inch pots; medium, in six- to eight-inch pots; or large, in pots over ten inches. Each category requires special potting techniques. But before you start to repot, make sure all containers are clean and have drainage holes, and soil is dry and on hand. Also, for any size plants with spines, wear gloves, or encircle plants with strips of folded newspaper.

Remove plants from small containers by first rapping the edges of the pots against a table or wooden shelf to loosen the plants. Never pull or grab plants from soil. Next put on gloves or drape a heavy cloth or wadded newspaper over the plants and wiggle them. The idea is to gently tease the plants from their pots. Small plants should come out easily.

To remove medium-sized plants, tap the bases of the pots against a solid surface to loosen the plants. Do this several times with plants in five- or six-inch pots. If you still have trouble removing the plants, insert a wooden blunt-nosed stick between the soil and the edges of the pots. Poke the stick in and out of each pot, around the diameter of the soil line. Then, with gloves on, grab the top of the plant and gently tease it from the old soil.

Large plants are almost impossible to lift because of their weight, so first hit the sides of the containers with a rubber mallet. Then use the potting stick and try to lift the plants out of their old soil. If the plants have been in their pots for several years, these methods may not extricate the plants, in which case you should go ahead and break the pots with a hammer. This is *not* foolish; it is better to destroy pots than plants, and I guarantee that playing tug-of-war with plants will destroy them. Use the broken pieces

as drainage-hole covers.

Once your small, medium, or large plants are out of their old soil, crumble away all the old soil from the roots. Do this gently by combing your fingers through the soil. If you notice any dead (brown) roots, judiciously cut them off. Never cut more than you must; leave some of the rootball soil intact.

Now prepare the new containers: put in some broken pieces of clay pots over the drainage holes and add a mound of soil to each pot. Put the plants in the soil and center them; if they look too high, take out some soil; if they look too low, add soil. Fill in and around the plants with soil, adding enough soil until the soil level is one or two inches from the tops of the pots, and tap the pots on a solid surface to settle the soil. Next, with your thumb or a blunt-edged stick, press down soil to eliminate any air pockets—you want the soil to be firm but not tightly packed.

If the plant is spiny and thus apt to hurt your hand, put soil in a newspaper chute or kitchen funnel and funnel the soil around the plant. Then rap the bottom of the pot on a table to settle the loose soil and add more soil. Finish by pressing the soil in place with a long wooden stick.

### EIGHT EXTRA HINTS

1. A very vertical plant should be potted in a container whose diameter is half the height of the plant and whose depth is greater than its width.

2. Globelike cactus needs a container about two inches wider in diameter than the plant's diameter.

3. Always use dry soil for potting or repotting because moist soil can cause crown rot.

4. Many cacti species are damaged by excessive moisture. To prevent rotting, replace the top inch of soil with one-half inch of crushed gravel so that the base of the plant is not in contact with the potting soil.

5. Do not water plants immediately after repotting them. Let them dry out for two to four days and then water sparingly the first two weeks. This allows broken roots to heal instead of rotting from excessive moisture.

6. Repot succulents or cacti in spring or fall because in those seasons the weather is good, and plants have a chance to regain vigor quickly. Summer and winter repottings put plants at a disadvantage because of extremely hot or very cold weather.

7. Small plants can go about a year without repotting; medium-sized plants should be repot-

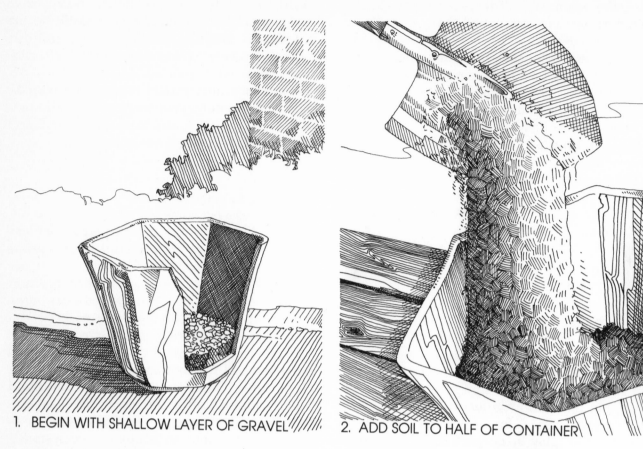

1. BEGIN WITH SHALLOW LAYER OF GRAVEL

2. ADD SOIL TO HALF OF CONTAINER

3. WITH CACTUS IN BURLAP, INSERT IN POT (SUPPORT CACTUS VERTICALLY)

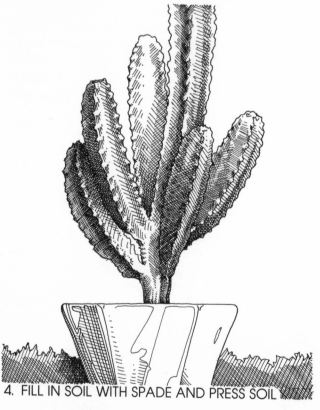

4. FILL IN SOIL WITH SPADE AND PRESS SOIL

# POTTING A LARGE CACTUS

ted every eighteen months; and large plants should be repotted every third year.

8. Very tall cacti with shallow root systems should be propped up with sticks or pieces of rock at the base. Try to make these props as unobtrusive as possible.

## Grooming

All plants should be groomed, but luckily succulents and cacti need less maintenance than most plants. Be sure to turn plants occasionally so that all sides are exposed to bright light. Never let faded flowers or decayed leaves remain on the soil because they can contribute to fungus diseases. If part of a plant becomes brown and surgery is necessary, do it immediately, before the disease or ailment spreads to other parts of the plant. To remove a branch, stem, or column, use a sterile knife (run a match flame over the knife to sterilize it). Make a clean cut, and then rub the cut with charcoal to help seal it.

Another important part of grooming, and one which seldom gets attention, is to keep plants free of dust and soot. Large cacti, especially after a few months indoors, accumulate thin layers of soot and dust on them. It is a good idea to keep this dust off of plants not only to maintain their attractiveness, but also to keep the pores of the plant open and exposed to air. Too much dust can contribute to disease in a plant if conditions are bad.

How do you dust a cactus? With an artist's paintbrush. Use a long-handled, inexpensive paintbrush with soft bristles (available at art stores) and carefully stroke off dust and dirt from in between spines and crevices of cacti. Many cacti have gnarled growth and the accumulation of dirt should be removed periodically. Dry brushing your plant will greatly contribute to its health and looks. It is a cultural step that should not be overlooked.

## Moving Large Plants

Moving large plants can be a problem. Just how to do this without straining your back is a prime consideration. Also, many columnar cacti are fragile; the weight of the stems sometimes causes them to break in moving—something to be avoided.

A good time to move plants is after repotting, and then it is best done by using plant trolleys (these can be found at nurseries or you can make one with four pieces of wood crisscrossed and casters attached). Without the trolley a plant, say in a sixteen-inch tub, requires two people to move it. Even with two people some rules must be observed. First, lift the plant pot vertically; if you tilt it, a columnar cactus can either uproot itself or simply break off at mid-point. Second, if you are manually moving a plant do it slowly step by step and grasp the pot rim firmly; one slip and bang—there goes the plant. Third, always have the new location cleared and ready for the plant.

# Five ❋ Indoor Decoration

There are innumerable ways in which succulents and cacti provide cheer and accent in the home. The kitchen-window garden is perhaps most popular because plants look good in kitchens, and many people spend hours there. Bedrooms and recreation rooms are other places for a few favorite cacti and succulents, and of course floor-sized plants are stunning accents in living rooms and dining areas. Small cacti and succulents on tables and desks are favorite accents, and fascinating and charming dish gardens create total lilliputian scenes. Succulents and cacti will survive anywhere in the home and will add an emphatic touch. You could not ask for better decoration.

## Window Gardens

Cacti and succulents are some of the most suitable houseplants for windows because most of them are small and compact and do not need much space. A dozen Rebutias, Parodias, and Lobivias can easily find happiness in an average window and create a pleasant garden. The window is of course the ideal place for plants because of light. To set up a window arrangement, you can just use a few shelves. Be sure that acrylic or glass shelves are thick (one-quarter inch) and place them on suitable side brackets or ledges of wood. Glass stores will cut shelves to order. This shelf arrangement is inexpensive and accommodates a dozen or so small plants. Commercial window-shelf kits are somewhat flimsy. It is much better to install your own shelves so that you can accurately set them into specific spaces. And the handmade look is always more appealing than the commercial look.

You can also try plant stands in front of windows. Generally these are multitray units with pedestal bases; each plant occupies one tray. Try to buy a plant stand that has perforated or grilled trays so air circulates at the bottom of the pot to help dry out saturated soil. It is especially important that cacti and succulents not have wet roots. Pedestals which accommodate one plant placed near windows put plants in an orderly fashion indoors. Try a group of three pedestals and use one medium- to large-sized plant on each pedestal.

Hanging cacti and succulents, such as *Sedum morganianum* (Burro's Tail), Rhipsalis, and *Oscularia deltoides,* are beautiful in front of windows. You will need containers with wire hangers, chain or monofilament wire, and an eye bolt. Put the eye bolt into the ceiling, attach the wire or chain to the bolt, and then hang the pot from the wire or chain. One word of caution: potted plants are heavy, so be sure all ceiling bolts are well secured. Always hang plants at eye level in groups of three; one plant looks out of place. (See Chapter 6 for more information.)

### SUCCULENTS FOR WINDOW PLANTS

A wide variety of growth forms and foliage colors

is represented by the plants in this list.

*Aeonium atropurpureum.* Interesting form; dark maroon leaves in flattened rosette growth.

A. 'Ballerina.' Sticky leaves edged in white; rosette growth. Oddity.

*A. canariense.* Large flattened rosette of apple green leaves.

*A. spathulatum.* Branching plant; light green leaf rosettes on woody stems.

*A. urbicum.* A natural hybrid; rosettes of shiny green leaves on a single trunk.

*Agave filifera* (Thread Plant). Decorative, narrow, olive green leaves bear loose, curled threads at the margins.

*A. horrida.* Rosette to twenty inches in diameter; leaves dark glossy green with sharp marginal spines.

*A. picta.* Narrow, pale green leaves with white margins; small black teeth.

*A. victoriae-reginae.* Striking plant with olive green leaves beautifully penciled with white edges.

*Aloe aristata* (Lace Aloe). Stemless. Tight rosette of thick, dark leaves; soft, white, short spines.

*A. nobilis* (Golden-Spined Aloe). Pointed green leaves are edged with irregular white teeth; plant is a rosette on a short stem.

*A. polyphylla* (Spiral Aloe). Rosette to twenty inches across, gray-green sickle-shaped leaves, dark brown at tip.

*A. striata* (Coral Aloe). Stiff, pointed, gray-green leaves about one-half inch wide, with narrow, pinkish edge; rosette growth on short trunk.

*A. variegata* (Partridge Breast or Tiger Aloe). Wavy bands of white markings on green leaves.

*Beaucarnea recurvata* (Pony Tail Plant). Globular, with arching leaves in rosette habit. Easily grown; unique.

*Bowiea volubilis* (Sea Onion). A pale green ball up to five inches in diameter with long, thin, twining stems that function as leaves. A real oddity.

*Caralluma pillansii.* Fleshy, deeply scalloped leaves, mottled with purple. Oddity.

*Cotyledon ladysmithiensis.* Dull green furry leaves; small, charming plant.

*C. undulata* (Silver Crown). Broad, showy leaves, beautifully fluted.

*Crassula arborescens* (Silver Dollar). Large silvery leaves with red margins and spots.

*C. argentea* (Jade Plant). Bright green rounded leaves suffused with red, shrubby growth.

'Crosby's Compact' is a fine hybrid.

*C. barbata.* Shrublike, branching from base. Green two-inch rosette with long white hairs. Likes sandy soil.

*C. cooperi.* Low growing with narrow green leaves dotted red; dainty plants form mats of growth.

*C. deltoidea* (Silver Beads). Low growing with fleshy, white, triangular leaves.

*C. erosula* 'Campfire.' Oval-shaped leaves; bronze-orange coloring. Bushlike.

*C. falcata.* Green fleshy leaves and masses of fiery red flowers.

*C. perforata variegata.* Angular leaves on stalks symmetrically spaced; reddish hue.

*Echeveria derenbergii* (Painted Lady). Thick, pale green rosette with red leaf margins.

*E. elegans.* Silver-blue rosette; pink flowers.

*E. haageana.* Loose, open rosette; leaves edged with pink.

*E. linguaefolia.* Loose rosette of pale green leaves; yellow flowers.

*E. pulvinata* (Plush Plant). Round, hairy leaves; red flowers.

*Euphorbia aerugnosa.* Never grows more than six inches; thin, blue-green stems; yellow flowers.

*E. clavarioides truncata.* Low growing, dense cushion of young branches; tiny, deciduous leaves.

*E. lactea.* Many-branched plant; the branches have three to four angles, spines, and whitish central stripe.

*E. milii splendens* (Crown of Thorns). Spiny stems with tiny, dark green leaves; bright red flowers.

*E. obesa* (Basketball Plant). A multicolored ribbed globe. Exquisite.

*Gasteria batesiana.* White, flecked, tongue-shaped leaves. Tufted growth.

*G. verrucosa* (Ox Tongue). Tapered pink and purple leaves with white warts.

Graptophyllum 'Aphrodite.' Similiar to Sedums; trailing rosettes.

*Haworthia angustifolia.* Light green rosettes of pointed leaves.

*H. tessellata.* Checkered lines on glossy, green, pointed leaves; rosette growth.

*H. truncata.* Dark green to brownish leaves with truncated ends. Needs warmth.

*Hoodia gordoni.* Numerous stems; branched, gray-green ribbed body.

*Huernia primulina.* Thick green stems covered with green or purplish spines; star-shaped flowers.

*Kalanchoe daigremontiana.* Stalked leaves of

shiny green running to a point; flecked on undersides.

*K. fedtschenkoi.* Blue-green leaves clustered at top of stems; brownish-pink flowers.

K. 'Rose Leaf.' Soft velvety gray to green-brown leaves.

*K. tomentosa* (Panda Plant). Tapered, white felt leaves covered with brown dots.

*Pachyphytum oviferum* (Moonstones). White powdery leaves; stemmy plant.

*P. viride.* Handsome bronze leaves three inches long.

*Portulacaria afra* (Elephant Bush). Bushy in growth; small, glossy, green leaves on red stems.

*Sansevieria trifasciata* 'Golden Hahnii.' Rosette; dark green leaves laced with yellow.

*Sedum adolphi* (Golden Sedum). Short, fleshy, yellow-green leaves tinged red; sprawling plant.

*S. multiceps.* Miniature "tree" with needle-like, dark green leaves; yellow flowers.

*S. oxypetalum.* Deciduous with peeling, papery bark; very slow growing.

*S. sieboldii.* Cascading plant with solitary stems, covered with wedge-shaped leaves lined in red.

*Stapelia gettleffii.* Slender, erect, green stems angled with soft hairs; yellowish-green flowers.

*S. gigantea* (Starfish Flower). Stout, club-shaped stems; pale yellow blossoms with red-brown lines.

*S. revoluta.* Upright grower with ribbed stems; distinctive star-shaped flowers.

*S. variegata.* Finger-like stems with spotted, star-shaped flowers.

*S. youngii.* Conical, tufted, green stems; large purple-and-green flowers.

## CACTI FOR WINDOW GARDENS

Most of these species have flowers which are quite large in proportion to the plants; often the spines are colorful as well. Most cacti flower in summer.

*Astrophytum capricorne* (Goat's Horn Cactus). Green globe with silver markings; three-inch flowers are yellow with red throats.

*A. ornatum* (Star Cactus). Globular to columnar ribbed plants; both spines and blooms are yellow.

*Cephalocereus palmeri* (Woolly Torch Cactus). Hardy plant with short, blue-green spines and tufts of white, woolly hair; columnar to branching.

*C. polyanthus* (Aztec Column). Slow growing, columnar with fluted ribs, yellow-brown spines.

*C. senilis* (Old Man Cactus). Ribbed, columnar growth; spines hidden in long white hairs.

*Chamaecereus sylvestri* (Peanut Cactus). Dense clusters of short green branches; red blooms.

*Cleistocactus baumannii* (Scarlet Bugler Cactus). Stiff stems topped with white spines; long blooming period of bright red, tubular flowers.

*C. strausii* (Silver Torch). Columnar clustering variety, silver-haired; dark red flowers.

*Coryphantha poselgerana.* Blue-green, warty growth clusters, long stiff spines; large reddish-purple flowers.

*Echinocactus grusonii* (Golden Barrel). Straight, sharp, yellow spines; with age develops a crown of yellow wool.

*Echinocereus baileyi.* Columnar growth with white spines; open-faced flowers are generally yellow.

*E. dasyacanthus* (Rainbow Cactus). Small columnar plant covered with soft spines; large yellow blossoms.

*E. ehrenbergii.* Stem erect, free-branching from base with slender, glassy, white spines; purple-red flowers.

*E. reichenbachii* (Lace Cactus). Small, heavily spined plant with red-and-yellow flowers.

*Epiphyllum* 'Conway's Giant.' Scalloped green leaves; oval red flowers.

*E. crenatum.* Beautiful six-inch white flowers.

E. 'Padre.' Five-inch pinkish-white flowers.

*Ferocactus histrix.* Large dark green globe with ribs; many sharp spines.

*Gymnocalycium andrea* X. *G. baldianum.* Dark bluish-green globe plant; ribbed.

*G. anisitsii.* Dark green ribbed globe; stiff spines. Pink flowers.

*G. camarpense.* Dark green globe; stiff spines. Greenish flowers.

G. 'Great Chin.' Sculptured body; rich green color; large spines.

*G. mihanovichii* (Chin Cactus). Grafted plants available in several colors.

*Hamatocactus hamatacanthus.* Dark green globe; ribbed, greenish-yellow flowers.

*Lobivia callianthus.* Tiny elongated globe; brilliant pink flowers.

*Mamillopsis senilis.* Gray-green globe with white hair; two-inch red flowers.

*Mammillaria bocasana* (Powder Puff or Snowball Cactus). Clustering growth; hooked central spine covered with white hair; small yellow flowers.

*M. celsiana.* Flat, orbicular, bluish-green body; fiery carmine flowers.

*M. compressa.* Grayish-green flat globe, almost elongated; rosy pink flowers.

*M. conspicua.* Spines tipped black surrounded with white spines; rose flowers.

*M. fera-rubra.* Heavily spined globe; small fiery red flowers in circle formation.

*M. guelzowiana.* Very hairy globe with hooked spines; two-inch red flowers.

*M. microcarpa.* Spiny globe with pink flowers.

*M. roseocentra.* Globular; grows two to three inches in diameter; white and rose red spines.

*M. schwarzii.* Woolly, hairy, white globe; tiny whitish-yellow flowers.

*Melocactus matanzanus* (Turk's Cap). Apple green body, heavily ribbed with spines; orange crown.

*Notocactus haselbergii* (Scarlet Ball). An early spring bloomer, globular growth covered with soft white spines; bright red blossoms.

*N. magnificus.* Dark green ribbed globe; very spiny.

*N. mammulosus* (Lemon Ball). Globular ribbed plant, gray to brown in color with short spines; yellow flowers.

*N. ottonis* (Indian Head). Clustering globular plant with bristly red-brown spines; yellow flowers.

*N. schumannianus* (Paraguay Ball). Globular growth, slanting at the top, with deep orange spines; yellow blooms.

*N. scopa* (Silver Ball). Globular, ribbed, and covered with soft white spines; yellow flowers.

*Opuntia basilaris* (Beaver Tail Cactus). Upright blue-green growths form compact pads; withstands low temperatures; blooms range from pink to carmine.

*O. bigelovii* (Teddy Bear Cactus). Branching plant; elongated stems covered with white hairs.

*O. microdasys* (Bunny Ears). A favorite house plant; Mexican dwarf species with flat, oblong, spineless pads covered by tufts of golden bristles.

*O. vestita* (Old Man Opuntia). Small very hairy leaves that are deciduous; red flowers. Can grow to twenty-four inches.

*Parodia aureispina* (Tom Thumb Cactus). Small globular plant with golden spines; yellow flowers.

*P. bueneckeri.* Apple green globe; abundant small red flowers.

*P. microthele.* Dark green globe; spiny; yellow flowers.

*P. rubiflora.* Bright green globe; soft yellow spines; pretty red flowers.

*P. sanguiniflora* (Crimson Parodia). Small, white-spined species; globular, with red flowers.

*Rebutia muscula (nivea)* (Red Crown). Clustering, globular growth with green heads; large brick red flowers.

*R. senilis* (Fire Crown). Dark green plant covered with a mass of snow white spines; blooms abundantly in brilliant red.

*Rhipsalis paradoxa* (Link Cactus). Flat green leaves with sawtooth edges; tiny white flowers.

*Schlumbergera bridgesii* (Easter Cactus). Dark green flattened, scalloped stems; pink or red terminal flowers. Also called Christmas Cactus.

*Zygocactus bridgesii* (Christmas Cactus). This is generally called the Christmas Cactus and has trailing flattened green stems and bright red or rose red flowers. *Z. truncatus* is sometimes referred to under the same common name, but is technically the Thanksgiving Cactus.

## Desk and Table Plants

Small succulents and cacti make fine desk and table plants when they are away from light and are set into decorative ceramic pots, or cachepots. (Note: plant in a clay pot and then put the clay pot into the cachepot.) However, plants away from the light will not grow as well as those in brightness; therefore, every month or so alternate plants for best results.

For table and desk plants, choose species that are really distinctive. For example, a small *Agave stricta* is unique and handsome, or select a Echinocereus, with showy flowers, or a Echinopsis, which has distinctive globular or cylindrical shape and ribs. Miniatures like Rebutias, Parodias, and Lobivias offer dramatic flowers and are perfect for a table or desk. You want something showy and different to captivate the eye because table and desk plants are always on display. Select plants from preceding window-garden lists.

## Floor Plants

Very large plants—the treelike specimens—are often used in place of a piece of furniture, and often they cost as much. But these dramatic giants are very desirable room accents. For example, tall columnar cacti like Trichocereus or large rosette-shaped Agaves look like carved stone sculptures. And at night, any properly lighted specimen cacti or succulents will create handsome silhouettes on ceilings.

Before you select a floor plant, decide whether you want vertical or horizontal emphasis in the room. For example, if your room is crowded, a large ball cactus like *Echinocactus grusonii* or a branching cactus like an Opuntia would be more in keeping with the furnishings than a giant columnar cactus. Tall plants should be used in more spacious areas.

Generally, most succulents and cacti are well suited to almost any room decor. Whether your home is contemporary or traditional, these plants blend well with surroundings and create a handsome picture. Texture and form are so versatile in these families that there is practically a plant for every decorating situation.

Borzicactus. A genus name that covers several genera; usually slender, branching plants, columnar or prostrate, with beautifully colored spines.

*Carnegiea gigantea* (Giant Saguaro). Handsome curving branches; angular and vertical.

Cephalocereus. Many different species; sometimes known as Pilocereus. Generally branching tall plants.

*C. dybowskii* is erect and slender to twelve feet, cylindrical and covered with white wool.

*Cereus hildmannianus*. Very tall, branching and columnar. Stunning room accent.

*C. peruvianus* (Apple Cactus or Peruvian Torch). Treelike and massive. *C. peruvianus* 'Monstrosus' is ribbed and somewhat contorted; dark green. Unique accent.

*Cleistocactus strausii* (Silver Torch). Erect plant; bold and big.

*Echinocactus grusonii* (Golden Barrel). Can grow four feet around with golden spines; makes a bold statement. Use low tubs.

*Euphorbia ingens*. Tall, green, columnar cacti, ribbed; branching habit.

*E. lactea*. Not a cactus but close enough. This one has angular contorted ribs, green-brown with spines.

*Furcraea gigantea*. Rosette of shiny green; narrow spiny leaves to seven feet.

*Lemaireocereus marginatus*. Treelike and sculptural; small stiff spines. Easy to grow.

*L. thurberi* (Organ Pipe Cactus). A ribbed, columnar giant, branching and growing to great heights. Purplish-green with black spines.

*Lophocereus schottii* 'Monstrosus' (Whisker Cactus). A ribless, spineless apple green giant with knobs and bumps. Likes warmth.

*Opuntia basilaris* (Beaver Tail Cactus). Oval pads of soft green; nearly spineless. Fine rugged accent for contemporary rooms. Several species suitable as room accents.

*Trichocereus glottsbergii*. Columnar; small and stout; prominent spines.

*T. schickendantzii*. Organ-type cactus, dark green column, white night-blooming flowers.

*T. spachianus* (Torch or White Torch Cactus). Strong, short, columnar growth; short spines and white flowers. Easy to grow.

## Dish Gardens

Cacti and succulent dish gardens can be unattractive if the marriage of plant material and landscaping is not done correctly. It takes a skilled hand to create a harmonious dish garden, but it can be done. And it is worth doing because once set up, dish gardens live for many years and rarely outgrow their containers, as do other houseplants when used in miniature scenes. You can duplicate specific terrains, such as deserts or woodlands, or just arrange plants one next to the other in a pleasing design. The idea is to put together a grouping of plants that appeals to the eye and catches the beauty of the outdoor scene.

Your first attempts at dish gardens will probably be anything but attractive because you need experience and an eye for proportion and scale. But stick with it because after your first few dish gardens you will get the idea.

The scene can be one you have seen in nature or in a photograph. The main premise is to use plants that have forms which mesh with each other. Horizontal and vertical accents must be used, and some rocks strategically placed always help. Rather than a flat terrain, which is uninteresting, use a slightly hilly landscape because this creates movement and visual beauty. Design the garden with an eye toward balance and scale, proportion and harmony. What you want is a totally pleasing picture.

For containers, use shallow bonsai pots (sold at nurseries) or any shallow five- to six-inch tray or box. Usually these containers do not have drainage holes, so you must take special care when watering plants. To prepare your dish garden, put in a one-quarter-inch layer of thinly crushed gravel at the bottom of the container. Next, sprinkle in some charcoal chips, and then place soil to about one-half inch of the top of the container. Select small plants and place them strategically until you come upon a pleasing arrangement. If a plant does not look good in one place, move it around until everything is to your liking. Water dish gardens about twice a week in spring and summer but not the rest of the year. Do not feed plants, because you want them to stay small. These miniature scenes will be closely scrutinized, so use handsome and healthy plants. Put dish gardens on windowsills, tables, or desks.

Dish-garden plants include:

*Adromischus maculatus* (Calico Hearts or Leopard Spots). Thick, flat leaves marked with chocolate brown.

*Aloe haworthioides*. Bright green leaves with small, sharp teeth; red flowers.

*A. plicatilis* (Fan Aloe). Shrubby; leaves arranged in two rows; gray-green with horny edges.

*Anacampseros alstonii*. Turnip-like growth, squatty. Oddity.

*Ariocarpus trigonus* (Living Stone). Fleshy, gray-green rosettes.

*Crassula tetragona* (Midget Pink). Dark green pointed leaves in four rows on stiff stems.

*Faucaria tigrina* (Tiger's Jaws). Low rosette of fleshy, triangular leaves; white teethlike spines.

*Gymnocalycium saglione*. Corky green body; pale pink flowers.

*Haworthia fasciata* (Zebra Haworthia). Dark green leaves banded in white.

*Pachyphytum oviferum* (Moonstones). Thick, fleshy, egg-shaped leaves, pink.

*P. viride*. Bronze egg-shaped leaves; branched.

*Pachypodium densiflorum*. Branching, deep green leaves; brown stems.

*Parodia camarguensis*. Beautiful green globe; orange-red flowers.

*Peperomia arifolia grandis*. Oval, fleshy, bright green leaves.

*Rebutia fiebrigii*. Tiny green globe; scarlet flowers.

*R. krainziana*. Small green globe; red flowers.

*Sedum hintonii*. Dwarf habit; small furry leaves on branched stem.

*Sempervivum ciliatum rubrum*. Small rosettes, green with rose tint.

*S. soboliferum*. Pale green rosettes one inch across.

63. Greenhouse Culture

A choice collection of Echeverias and Agaves is seen here in a California greenhouse. The structure is of fiber glass and has no facility for winter heat. The cool winter temperatures add greatly to the health and vigor of these plants.

64. Epiphyllum 'Padre'

This is one of the older Orchid Cactus hybrids, and it produces an amazing number of five-inch flowers in the spring. The plant requires little care, is spineless, and makes a beautiful hanging-basket specimen.

65. *Aeonium arboreum* 'Schwarzkopf' (also 'Zwartkop')
    Canary Islands

This startling mutation from the plain green form first appeared in Europe and is known both as 'Zwartkop' (Dutch) and 'Schwarzkopf' (German), meaning 'Black Head.' Brilliant sun intensifies the dark maroon, almost black, coloration of the leaves. The plants grow to approximately two feet tall, producing a spectacular group of rosettes.

66. *Notocactus rutilans*
    Argentina

The Pink Ball Cactus produces one and one-half inch flowers with an incredible silken texture. This vigorous species flowers when very young.

67. *Mammillaria microcarpa*
    Southwestern United States; Sonora

The common Fishhook Cactus may grow as a single plant or as a clump of several, usually to about six inches in height. The three-quarter-inch blossoms may be produced in great profusion, as in this specimen which has twenty-two blossoms open at one time.

68. *Hoya carnosa* 'Tricolor'

The thick, waxy leaves of this Hoya are brilliantly colored in this recently introduced cultivar. It grows well in a hanging basket or trained on a trellis. The soil must dry out between waterings, and the long tendrils should not be pinched, as the waxy, jewel-like flowers are produced near the growing tips.

69. *Parodia rubiflora*
    Argentina

Some of the Parodias come from elevations as high as thirteen thousand feet, and, as a group, they tend to be quite undemanding in their culture. The spiral arrangement of ribs in the one seen here is typical of many. This pattern creates a very decorative plant even when it is out of bloom.

70. *Kalanchoe blossfeldiana*
    Madagascar

Selective breeding of this succulent has resulted in a popular florist's plant with incredibly brilliant, long-lasting flowers. There are several strains with other colors. The dark green, shiny foliage is also very attractive.

71. *Gymnocalycium mihanovichii*
    Paraguay

This startling mutation possesses almost no chlorophyll and, as a result, must be grafted on to the root stock of another cactus in order to survive. The existence of these bizarre mutations, in hues of red, yellow, pink, orange, green, and black, is rather precarious, but they are produced in great quantities, particularly in Japan, and are readily available from dealers.

72. *Crassula perforata variegata*
    South Africa

This perfect specimen of erect stems, branching from the base, is a mutation from the normal green variety. The beautifully variegated leaves make it a most desirable succulent. The vertical stems of this specimen are not typical, as it normally tends to trail, making it a good choice for hanging baskets.

73. *Mammillaria bocasana*
    Mexico

The Powder Puff or Snowball Cactus forms a mound of little globes covered with silken hair and hooked, brown spines. It produces abundant flowers and is one of the easier Mammillarias to grow. However, it must be watered cautiously, especially in the winter.

74. *Lobivia callianthus*
    Argentina

The genus name is an anagram of Bolivia, which is the home of most of the species. They come from high altitudes and are easy plants to grow. They are known for their very large, brilliantly colored blossoms.

75. *Trichocereus auricolor*
    Peru

This is a vigorous, high-altitude plant that branches freely from the base, producing stems about three inches thick. It produces a profusion of blossoms.

76. *Echinocereus engelmannii*
    Southwestern United States

The hardy Strawberry or Hedgehog Cactus grows to about one foot in height and is covered with stiff, white, yellow, brown, or gray spines. The red-purple flowers, two to three inches in diameter, are produced in March and April.

77. *Rebutia krainziana*
    Andes of South America

This neat plant, with one-inch flowers, is an ideal species. It grows easily and requires no special care other than well-drained soil and a cool, dry, winter rest.

78. *Mammillaria swinglei*
    Mexico

This plant is native to the coastal areas of Sonora and grows well with intense summer heat. It may reach eight inches in height, with one and one-half inch blossoms.

79. Echeveria 'Afterglow'

This hybrid possesses the powdery leaves of *Echeveria subrigida,* which is the mother plant, and the pinkish-lavender color of Echeveria 'Whitei Rose.' It is a vigorous plant, but produces offsets rarely. The blossoms, sometimes insignificant in Echeverias, are unusually large and are deep orange-red in color. Like many other leaves which have a heavy deposit of powder, these are easily marred, ruining the beauty of the plant.

63

64

66

68

69

70

74

75

76

77

78

79

# Six ❋ Cacti and Succulents in the Air

In Chapter 5, I briefly discussed cacti and succulents as plants for hanging containers. Gardens in the air are so popular, and rightly so, that this chapter is devoted to them. And in the world of cacti and succulents there are many plants that are outstanding performers in hanging containers. A very common and popular houseplant is the Christmas Cactus that is stunning in baskets. Some overlooked plants such as *Senecio rowleyanus* and some Sedums are equally good in containers suspended from ceilings.

## Gardens in the Air

Gardens in the air look good and utilize otherwise useless space. At eye level and near windows, plants in hanging containers have maximum light and air circulates around the pot, which helps many plants. There are indeed several advantages to growing plants in the air, and that is why this kind of indoor gardening is so popular.

However, plants at eye level are always on display and need more trimming and grooming than plants at windows. They also require more care—in good light the plants grow faster and need more water and more frequent potting. This is especially true of cacti and succulents, which need more moisture and feeding than plants in other indoor locations.

Soil for hanging plants should be evenly moist all year except in December and January, when the plants can be grown somewhat dry but never

so dry that soil gets cakey. Trim basket plants; shaping is necessary when you grow plants in the air. The plant should be symmetrical, neither lopsided nor growing in an ungainly manner. I trim cacti and succulents in hanging containers, snipping off an errant branch here and there. Also, I position plants differently about every three months so that all parts of the plant get light and growth is symmetrical.

## Containers

There is an array of hanging containers: some clay, some plastic, or some new materials which I cannot determine from looking at. No matter which container you select, get one that has an attached drain saucer or one to which a saucer can be attached for catching dripping water. If you simply use a standard clay pot without a saucer you must remove the plant from its mooring and take it to the sink for watering and that is a bother.

You will find hanging containers at nurseries as well as advertised in garden magazines. Use the ones that suit your needs (as long as they have facilities for a drip saucer or include one). I use clay pots and for drip pans the standard clay saucer under the pot. I buy the clip-on hangers and attach the saucer to the pot; sometimes the saucer is in the metal hanger and the pot is placed on the saucer. The weight of the pot keeps the saucer in place.

The old-fashioned wire baskets have their

uses too; plants grow rapidly in these because of the open space between the wires. Air gets to all parts of the plant and this stimulates good growth. However, with these wire baskets it is almost impossible to avoid water dripping on floors. If you have tile or brick floors where water on the surface is not a problem, then use the wire baskets. They are very inexpensive compared to standard pots. Pot wire baskets with a sheet of osmunda or sphagnum moss lining the container and then fill with soil.

## Potting Baskets

Use standard potting methods as described previously for planting hanging containers. However, pot two or three small plants to a container in a triangular pattern. This will give you symmetrical growth and the plant will not look lopsided. If plants are very tiny a fourth one can be used in the center. With three or four plants growing at the same rate the basket will fill out evenly and look handsome.

Never stick one plant in the center and expect any measure of beauty. This arrangement looks funny, and it takes years for the plants to fill out and cover the basket. With proper planting initially, the baskets in time become halos of color almost completely covered with plants. Many of my hanging containers are not visible; plants have covered the outside, cascading over the pot rim with trailing stems of beauty.

## Plants for Hanging Baskets

Practically any plant can be grown in a hanging container but some—trailing and cascading types—are better than others. Here is a partial list of some of the plants I have grown. You may try others too. Most plants, except columnar and globe-shaped, look attractive in hanging containers.

Aeonium hybrids. There are many in this group that make fine hanging plants. They have rosette-type growth and adapt well to hanging containers. Generally bright green to purple, they look like leafy roses. *A. pseudotabulae-forme* is especially handsome.

*Aporocactus flagelliformis* (Rattail Cactus). More beautiful than its name implies, this cascading stemmy plant bears bright, beautiful red or pink flowers. There are many vari-

eties and they are well worth growing.

*Ceropegia woodii* (String of Hearts). Long a favorite, this succulent has tiny heart-shaped leaves spaced about one inch apart on thin wiry stems. It is not as attractive as most hanging plants because by nature it never really bushes out to make a halo of color. If you do want to grow it in the air, use several plants to a pot.

*Crassula perforata* (String of Buttons). The leaves of this Crassula resemble tiny buttons closely packed next to each other. It is rarely grown as a hanging plant but makes a splendid show. Try it.

*Epiphyllum* hybrids (Orchid Cactus). These are the beauties of the Epiphyllum family with mammoth flowers and trailing stems. Most of the year they do not look like much but in summer they blaze with colorful bloom. They must be grown in a basket as pendant growth makes them unsuitable for desks or tables.

*Kleinia tomentosa* (Chalk Plant). With chalky finger-like growth, this is a handsome plant. It is blue-green in color and looks good in baskets. It makes a bushy, unusual accent and is highly recommended.

*Oscularia deltoides*. Small blue-gray branchlets and small pink flowers. Makes a somewhat bushy display.

*Othonna capensis* (Little Pickles). This succulent resembles its common name with tiny little pickle-like bright green leaves. It grows in a cascading fashion and makes an excellent hanging plant.

*Rhipsalis paradoxa* (Link Cactus). This is a natural trailing plant with green scalloped "leaves" (more like stems). It is not exceptionally handsome but grows easily and trailing stems can reach five feet. *R. caerulea* and *R. rhombea* are also suitable for baskets.

*Sedum morganianum* (Burro's Tail). This is probably the most popular succulent hanging plant; it is a natural trailer and has small beadlike bright green leaves on long stems. A mature specimen is a breathtaking sight because stems can trail to five feet. The stems are brittle, however, so be careful when handling this plant.

*Sedum stahlii* (Baked Beans). From its common name you can judge that the leaves of this plant look like small round beans and are produced on cascading stems. Somewhat similar to *S. morganianum*, it can in time grow into a beautiful hanging plant.

*Senecio rowleyanus* (Pea Plant). More an oddity

than a beauty, the Pea Plant appears like small green peas on delicate stems and has caught the public fancy. It is unusual and does make an attractive hanging.

*Zygocactus truncatus* (Christmas Cactus). Whether you call these Christmas or Easter cacti, or refer to them as Schlumbergera or Rhipsalidopsis, they make superior hanging plants. They are available at Easter, Christmas, and Thanksgiving and most have rose or red terminal flowers at the ends of cascading green stems (leaves). These make very handsome basket plants and grow lavishly in this way.

# Seven ✳ Cacti and Succulents Under Lights

Artificial light for houseplants has enabled people in homes and apartments to grow house-plants in areas that naturally do not get enough light. In fact, the boom of fluorescent plant lamps has been like a miracle: African Violets are now blooming in closets, orchids are flourishing under lamps, annuals and perennials are thriving in dismal back rooms, and on and on. Artificial light has become so popular that it is now recommended as a supplement to natural light at windows. No matter how you look at it, artificial light will help keep your cacti and succulents healthy and will increase their growth.

## Fluorescent Light Units

Most artificial light units—carts or shelves — are rarely handsome; they look like sterile growth chambers. And most light units can accommodate nothing taller than twenty-four- to twenty-eight-inch plants. There are many different types of tubular fluorescent lights, including Gro-Lux, by Sylvania; Vita Lite, by Duro Light; the standard commercial fluorescent lamps like Daybright and Cool.

There are now cone-shaped plant fixtures that hold standard-shaped bulbs which are designed to make plants grow. These fixtures are fairly attractive, and a few of them on walls or ceilings are good for plants in dark places. Nurseries and plant stores sell these plant-grow fixtures.

But generally, if you want an artificial light unit that looks good, you are going to have to make it yourself so that it blends into the living or dining room. It is not hard to make your own light setup but it does require some carpentry; a unit consists of a reflector at the top, plywood panels, and a bookcase-type of construction. Many books on artificial light feature construction drawings.

### SETUPS

You will need at least two 40-watt fluorescent tubes for a setup; the rule of thumb is twenty to thirty watts per square foot, with the plants two to three inches from the light source. What specific lamp you use is up to you. Gro-Lux and Vita Lite work fine, as do standard lamps, especially Daylight. Generally, for cacti and succulents, keep the lamps on fourteen to sixteen hours daily during the spring and summer, ten to twelve hours in the fall, and eight to ten hours in the winter. Note that these are average figures, so I urge you to experiment and keep records. Watch plant growth and adjust lights accordingly. (If you have many plants, I suggest you put the artificial light unit in a basement or other out-of-the-way area.)

You can also use standard incandescent lamps (reading bulbs) to furnish some light for plants. My kitchen fixtures are track-light systems with 150-watt floodlights. Two lights are aimed at the kitchen window; I must admit that the African Violets there far outbloom the ones across the room in indirect light. So even an incandescent lamp will do the job.

## Light and Plants

Many cacti species from deserts need strong light to prosper, and artificial light works well for these plants. Non-desert succulents such as Aloes, Haworthias, Crassulas, and Stapelias, for example, do not require intense light so do not need intense artificial light. Keep cacti species (those with spines) in the center of the lamp area (where light is the brightest) and succulent types at the ends of the lamps, where light is not too intense.

Generally, desert cacti should be placed two to four inches from the light source, but succulents are best positioned three to five inches from the light. The twelve- to fourteen-hour day-length is good for most succulents and cacti. But in fall begin to reduce the day-length so that by winter you are growing plants with eight to ten hours of light. Most succulents and cacti need somewhat of a rest during the cold months.

In February start increasing the day-length by allowing plants eleven to twelve hours and in mid-summer go back to the twelve- to fourteen-hour day.

## Care

The prime thing to remember when growing cacti and succulents under lights is that no matter what the setup, plants grow all year. This means you must give plants care all year. Plants grown under natural light go through a resting period in winter, at which time care is at a minimum, but this is not so when plants are grown under lights. Plants under lights will need somewhat more water, humidity, and feeding.

## Plants to Grow

You cannot grow all kinds of succulents and cacti under lights. Columnar type and large candelabra specimens just will not do. Generally, there is not enough space for these in light setups. It is best to concentrate on small and medium-sized plants and those that will be compact in an artificial light setup. These include a host of plants starting with Adromischus, small Agaves, small Aloes, Crassulas, Echeverias, Gasterias, Haworthias, Kalanchoes, Pachyphytums, Sedums, and Stapelias.

These are the plants that seem to thrive under lights while Lophocereus and Trichocereus and plants of this type do not do as well. Echinocactus, Mammillarias, Chamaecereus, Parodias, Lobivias, and Rebutias are ideal cacti for light growing. Forget scandent growers like Epiphyllums and Christmas Cactus types.

## Seed Under Lights

Growing seed under artificial light deserves a special section because seeds respond so well in this type of growing situation: growth is faster and conditions are more stable. The basic techniques of starting seed are explained in Chapter 8; the same methods and manner of handling seeds apply to artificial light growing.

To grow seed under lights you will need a reflector and one 40-watt Daylight lamp of a suitable length (twenty-four, thirty, thirty-six inches, and so on). Keep the light source six to eight inches from the seed bed and keep lights on for twelve to fourteen hours. Once seedlings sprout, you can increase light duration to sixteen to eighteen hours.

Be sure temperatures are between 75 and 80°F for seed germination, and keep the medium uniformly moist but never wet. Provide a good circulation of air; a small fan at low speed works well. To increase humidity, use a box setup, with lights under the ceiling and a plexiglass door at the front. By opening and closing the door you can regulate humidity.

A plywood propagating light box is simple to make. Use a baseboard, two sides, and a stable top. To the underside of the top attach lamp fixtures. Paint the inside of the box white. You can also propagate all kinds of plants and cuttings in this setup.

80. *Gasteria batesiana*
   South Africa

The six-inch-long leaves of this succulent assume beautiful red shadings in intense light when restraint is used in watering. The plant is slow growing, but produces enough offsets to eventually fill a pot.

81. Dish Garden of Haworthias
   South Africa

This container includes the following: (back row, left to right) *Haworthia tortuosa, Haworthia asperiuscula patagiata,* Haworthia (unnamed hybrid), and (front row, left to right) *Haworthia browniana, Haworthia translucens,* and *Haworthia bolusii.* Most Haworthias appreciate generous watering during the growing period and prefer partial shade. Too much sunlight burns them rather quickly.

82. *Agave schidigera* 'Taylori'
   Mexico

This beautiful two-foot rosette was found growing on a rocky outcropping at the eight-thousand-foot elevation in the Sierra Madre of western Mexico. Young specimens form admirable pot plants, remaining small for years. This particular species never forms offsets, and propagation is by seed only.

83. *Graptopetalum filiferum*
   Mexico

These tiny, one- to two-inch rosettes offset very freely and will form a beautiful mound which entirely covers the soil in a pot. Cultivation is simple, but a resting period in winter is necessary.

84. *Euphorbia lactea*
   India; Ceylon

This is a shrubby, slow-growing, warmth-loving species which is seen here as a ten-foot specimen. It has become naturalized in the West Indies and Florida. It is a very popular pot plant for cold climates.

85. *Aloe aristata*
   South Africa

The popular, small Lace Aloe is a beautiful stemless rosette of dark leaves with harmless, white, cartilaginous spines. It produces offsets, and propagation may also be achieved with leaf cuttings. The flowers are orange-red.

86. *Aloe haworthioides*
   Madagascar

This tiny, delicate, hairy plant collects moisture from the air in order to help sustain it in its dry habitat. It may grow to four or five inches in height and offsets freely to form a spectacular clump.

87. *Abromeitiella chlorantha*
   Argentina; Bolivia

There are a large number of succulent plants within the Bromeliad or Pineapple family, and this is one of the most satisfactory. The dainty plants, less than two inches in diameter, offset very freely and will form a solid carpet in a pot. The flowers are green.

88. *Caralluma pillansii*
   Cape Province

This freely branching plant reaches a foot in height and is beautifully mottled with purple. The flowers are reddish-gray spotted with red. It grows well with summer warmth and ample water. During the winter dormancy, water should be withheld almost totally in order to avoid rot. During this period tiny amounts of water, such as one tablespoon, may be given to prevent undue shriveling of the plant.

89. *Euphorbia candelabrum*
   Africa

This is a tall-growing plant which is used as a hedge in Africa and other tropical countries. Branching from the base, it is seen here as a ten-foot specimen. As with most Euphorbias, young specimens function well as small pot plants.

90. *Haworthia fasciata*
   South Africa

This is one of the most popular Haworthias because of its vigor and its great beauty. As in all the plants of this genus, the flowers are tiny and insignificant. Some growers remove the inflorescence as soon as it begins to appear, thus conserving energy for additional foliage growth and the production of offsets. The plants grow to four or five inches in height.

91. *Stapelia gigantea*
   South Africa

The carrion-like odor of these foot-wide flowers attracts blowflies which act as the pollinating agents. The blossoms of the Starfish Flower are pale yellow with delicate red-brown lines. This is a vigorous, easily grown pot plant seen here growing in the open ground in a warm, frost-free climate.

92. *Stapelia gettleffii*
   South Africa

This startling plant with velvety-hairy stems grows to ten or twelve inches in height. The flower is typically starfish-shaped, with an exotic combination of purple and yellow colors.

93. *Agave victoriae-reginae*
   Northern Mexico

This Agave is probably the most spectacular of all the Century Plant group. It is very slow growing, but, contrary to popular belief, does not require one hundred years in order to flower. Some Agaves may flower in as little as five years. Old specimens of victoriae-reginae may reach two feet in diameter. In its natural habitat it clings to steep, sometimes vertical, rocky slopes. Offsets are never formed, and propagation is by seed only. It is an admirable plant for pot culture.

94. *Bowiea volubilis*
   South Africa

The Sea Onion sits on top of the soil and produces long, thin tendrils during the summer growing season. Propagation is achieved by peeling separate scales from the green, lily-like bulb and laying them on slightly moist soil.

95. *Agave attenuata*
   Mexico

The soft, pale green leaves, with no spines whatsoever, make this a most desirable pot plant. It produces offsets in prodigious numbers, and small plants, as well as seeds, are produced on the bloom stalk. It is one of the commonest succulents for landscaping purposes in tropical and subtropical areas.

96. *Agave horrida*
Mexico

This succulent grows naturally on nearly soilless lava flows north of Cuernavaca, Mexico, but is photographed here growing happily in a California garden. Being slow growing, it is a satisfactory plant for pot conditions. The rosettes may reach two feet in diameter, but never produce offsets.

97. *Agave palmeri*
Arizona; New Mexico; Northern Mexico

This is a typical view in the *Agave palmeri* habitat of southeastern Arizona. The twenty-foot-tall inflorescence seen here signals the death of most individual plants in the Century Plant group. However, the species reproduces prolifically both by offsets and seeds.

98. *Carnegiea gigantea*
Southern Arizona; Northern Mexico

The fragrant, white, night-blooming blossom of the Giant Saguaro is the state flower of Arizona. This is one of the largest of all cacti, reaching heights of fifty feet after growing for, perhaps, two hundred years. Young specimens, with their beautiful brown spines, make interesting pot plants, but must have full sun.

99. *Agave tequilana*
Mexico

Fields of this large Agave are a common sight in certain areas of Mexico and Central America. As indicated by its species name, the fermented juice of the plant is used to produce tequila.

100. *Ariocarpus trigonus*
Mexico

This hard, fleshy rosette of a grayish-green color is well camouflaged in the desert areas where it grows. It possesses a thickened root which acts as a reservoir of moisture to carry it through long dry periods. The flowers are yellow.

101. *Opuntia bigelovii*
Southwestern United States

The Teddy Bear of the Arizona deserts is a beautiful plant to look at, but, of all cacti, it is perhaps the most fearsome. Each joint is detached at the slightest touch due to the barbed spines. The plant requires full, intense sun for good development. The difficulty of handling this cactus has more or less eliminated its use as a cultivated plant.

102. *Opuntia vestita*
Bolivia

This high-altitude cactus is completely clothed with harmless white hair and small leaves which disappear during the resting period. The plant grows to two feet, producing a clump, and the flowers are deep red.

103. *Agave angustifolia* 'Marginata'
Yucatan; Honduras?

A popular landscaping plant in tropical countries, this specimen is approximately thirty inches across. It also performs well as a potted plant. The origin of this plant is somewhat mysterious; apparently there is no official record of its native habitat. The tall succulent seen here growing in the background is *Euphorbia lactea*.

104. Gymnocalycium 'Giant Chin'

The white flowers, naked scaly buds, large spines, and sculptured body make a most interesting succulent for window culture. It is easily grown, and its rich green color makes it attractive even when not blooming.

105. *Agave filifera compacta*
Mexico

Almost as beautiful as *Agave victoriae-reginae,* this small plant, seen here growing in a California greenhouse, never becomes more than six inches in diameter. It produces offsets reluctantly and, because of this fact, is somewhat uncommon.

106. *Uebelmannia pectinifera*
Brazil

This unusual tropical cactus with a dark brown body comes from areas of high summer rainfall, where it grows in the company of Bromeliads. The flowers are yellow, and it grows as a solitary plant.

107. *Astrophytum myriostigma*
Mexico

The Bishop's Cap comes from the higher altitudes of central Mexico and is a vigorous and durable plant. Its spineless quality and its large pale yellow flowers make it a most desirable succulent. Old plants may become eight inches or more in diameter.

108. *Aloe nobilis*
Cape Province

Dark green leaves with horny, white teeth create a startling effect in this clustering plant. The rosettes may reach six to eight inches in diameter, and the flowers are red. It is somewhat slow growing, but is rather carefree in cultivation.

109. *Adromischus maculatus*
South Africa

The reddish-brown spots easily account for the common name Leopard Spots or Calico Hearts. This succulent remains small, with leaves up to two inches broad and long.

110. *Fenestraria rhopalophylla*
Southwest Africa

This miniature succulent, with translucent tips on the leaves, is commonly referred to as Baby Toes. In the harsh sunlight of its native country the entire plant is buried in the sand up to the "windowed" tips, which filter the intense illumination.

111. *Euphorbia clavarioides truncata*
South Africa

This low-growing plant forms a dense cushion of young branches with tiny, deciduous leaves at the tips. It is an ideal pot plant and will, in time, completely cover the soil.

112. *Aloe aristata montanum*
South Africa

There are many hybrids existing between *Aloe aristata* and various members of the Gasteria genus, which is very closely related. Many of those bigeneric hybrids closely resemble this vigorous plant. It grows very easily and rapidly and requires no special care. The rosettes are approximately six inches in diameter.

113. *Dyckia brevifolia*
Brazil

This vigorous, freely offsetting plant is one of the most widely grown succulents in the Bromeliad family. The thick-leafed rosettes may reach eight inches in diameter, and they produce orange flowers on a tall spike.

114. *Trichocereus schickendantzii*
    Northwest Argentina

This is one of the smaller species of the Organ Pipe type of cacti, and it branches freely from the base, producing a compact group of shiny, dark green columns. Coming from the high altitudes of the Andes, it is an easily grown plant and can withstand winter temperatures down to twenty degrees if it is kept dry during that period. It produces large, attractive white flowers. This specimen is growing as a greenhouse pot plant.

115. *Echinocereus pectinatus rigidissimus*
    Arizona

Seen from above, this young specimen of the Arizona Rainbow Cactus displays an interesting growth pattern in the spines. Older specimens possess a spine color varying from white to brown and pink, accounting for the common name. The flowers are large and vibrant pink in color.

116. *Agave filifera*
    Mexico

Seen from above, this complex arrangement of leaves and filaments creates an interesting mandala-like effect. The plant is very easily grown and reaches a diameter of eighteen inches. It produces many offsets.

117. *Begonia venosa*
    Brazil

The thick, heavily felted leaves of this Begonia clearly identify it as a succulent. It is a beautiful plant, with gray-green foliage, inflated, papery stipules at the leaf bases, and white flowers.

118. *Monvillea spegazzinii cristata*
    South America

This crested variety bears little resemblance to the normal species, but it is a spectacular cactus with its strong textures and pronounced sculptural effects. It requires a lighter soil and somewhat more shade and warmth than many cacti.

80

81

82

83

84

85

86

87

88

90

91

92

93

94

95

97

98

99

100

101

102

103

104

105

106

108    109

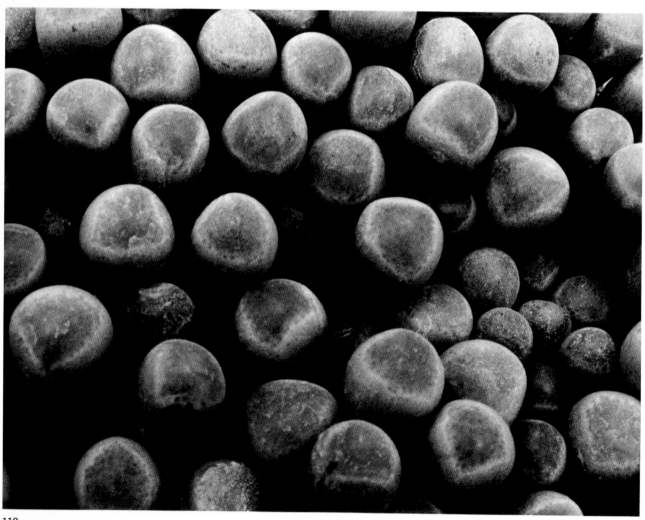

110

111

112      113

115

117

# Eight ❋ Propagating Techniques

Unlike most leafy houseplants, succulents and cacti bear more offsets. And many cacti and succulents can be multiplied easily by cuttings and divisions. In fact, between offsets and cuttings, you may find yourself with too many plants! Also, many cacti and succulents are so easy to grow from seed that if even half the seeds do not germinate, you will still have more than enough plants. Finally, grafting (growing one plant onto another), although not strictly a propagating technique, deserves mention.

Taking offsets, divisions, and cuttings requires little equipment and little cost. And sowing and grafting are fairly easy to do. Let us study the ways you can increase your supply of cacti and succulents.

## Cuttings

Propagating stem or leaf cuttings is perhaps the easiest way of getting new plants from succulents and cacti. Cuttings can be taken from a stem tip or a piece of stem that contains leaf nodes or from a whole leaf or part of a leaf. However, only succulents can be propagated by leaf cuttings; stem cuttings are fine for both cacti and succulents.

To propagate a leaf cutting, let the leaf dry in the air for a few days. Then place the leaf in a sterile growing medium like vermiculite or sand. Kalanchoes, Haworthias, and Gasterias are prime candidates for leaf propagation. Start the cuttings in a shallow five-inch tray with adequate drainage. Use a sandy well-drained soil mix—three parts sand to one part soil. Set the leaf cuttings in place so they are in contact with the soil but not embedded too deeply. Keep containers in bright light and be sure to keep the medium moist. Plumpness on new leaves is a good indication that roots are forming; this time can vary from weeks to months. Once roots are formed, put the individual plants in separate pots of soil.

Handle stem cuttings the same way, that is, use a shallow tray or box and sandy soil or vermiculite. Remove the bottom leaves, but retain some leaves at the top. Embed the cuttings. Put the tray or box in bright but not sunny light and keep soil evenly moist but never soggy. If you want to increase humidity, put a plastic tent over the top of the tray.

All cuts should be made cleanly with a sterile knife or razor blade; never break or tear leaves or stems from a plant. Always dry out the cuttings a few days before you try to root them; put them in a cool, well-ventilated area for a few weeks so they can scar over.

The best time to take cuttings is in spring or summer, which is when plants have finished their resting. Look for mature growth and take sizable cuttings. You can also root some cuttings in a jar of water; it does not always work, but sometimes it does.

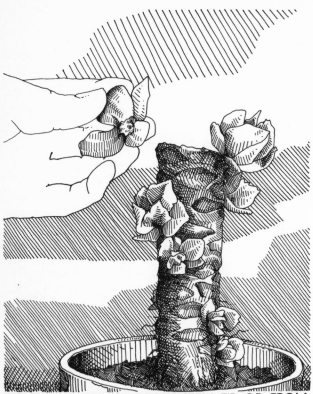

1. MAKE CUTTINGS FROM STEM TIP OR FROM STEM THAT CONTAINS LEAF NODES

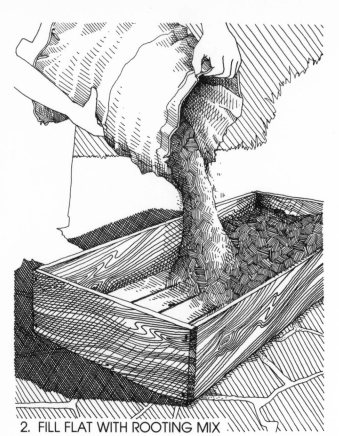

2. FILL FLAT WITH ROOTING MIX

3. SET CUTTINGS IN PLACE IN CONTACT WITH SOIL

4. WHEN ROOTS HAVE FORMED, PLANTS ARE READY TO BE POTTED INDIVIDUALLY

# CUTTINGS

1. CLUMPS OF MATURE SUCCULENTS CAN BE DI-VIDED INTO MORE NEW PLANTS

2. SEPARATE BY CUTTING

3. PUT NEW PLANTS IN SOIL MIXTURE

4. WATER COPIOUSLY

# DIVISIONS

1.   TAKE LEAF CUTTINGS FROM MATURE PLANTS

2.   SET LEAVES IN STERILE POTTING MIX

3. WHEN SMALL PLANTS APPEAR WITH ROOTS, CUT THEM OFF FOR POTTING

4.   SET SEEDLINGS IN CONTAINERS OF POROUS SOIL

# LEAVES

1. SLICE OFF TOP OF STOCK PLANT

2. TRIM DOWN SHOULDERS AND SCION

3. GROWTH RINGS OF STOCK AND SCION MUST BE SAME DIAMETER

4. PRESS PIECES TOGETHER AND SECURE WITH RUBBER BANDS

# HOW TO GRAFT CACTUS

## Offsets and Divisions

Offsets, or small plants, duplicates of the mother plant, appear at the base of succulents and cacti. Gently twist the offsets loose, or cut them with a sterile knife and start them in a sandy soil mix.

Any plant that grows in clumps—and several cacti do—can be increased by division. Sever the plant at the division point (the division point is quite easy to spot) using a sterile sharp knife. Take the plant from the pot and lay it on a table. Make a cut clean through the base and roots; pot the division separately.

## Cacti and Succulents from Seed

The slowest, but perhaps the surest, method of getting new cacti and succulents is to grow them from seed. Most plants produced from seed are healthier and more adaptable to growing conditions than plants produced by other propagation techniques. Buy packaged seed at nurseries and start the seed in spring. Wooden boxes or flats or wide shallow clay pots are good for seed sowing. A good growing medium is two parts soil, one part leaf mold, and two parts sand, or use vermiculite. The starting mix should be firmly but not tightly packed into the container. It should be porous and have air spaces so water can flow through it freely.

Embed large seed into the medium twice the depth of their own diameter; sprinkle fine seed on the surface of the soil. Keep seed trays in a warm place (78°F) while seeds are germinating. Put the trays in a shady place and cover them with a sheet of glass or plastic to ensure good humidity. If the covering shows condensation, let some air into the tray; otherwise seedlings may develop botrytis, a fungus disease. It is vital that during the germination period the temperature not fluctuate and that there are no drafts in the growing area.

Watering the seeds requires care; you cannot just dump water into the tray because it will push the seeds out of place. A gentle flow of water is the best method. Keep the medium uniformly moist, never soggy or dry. Some seeds, like Stapeliads, germinate in a week, but other seeds, especially those of cactus, may take several months. However, never give up on seeds, even if you have to wait a year, which is how long it takes some species to germinate.

When seeds sprout and leaves appear, give the plants a little more light and remove any coverings. Too much light can burn seedlings, but too little light may help to cause fungus to grow on the surface of the starting medium. Increase moisture and light as the leaves get larger. Once leaves are two to four inches high, water seedlings somewhat less; keep them just barely moist. After about six months, transfer the seedlings to individual pots.

When you transplant the seedlings, do it carefully. Do not rip them from the medium; tease them loose with a blunt-edged stick and take as much of the rootball as possible. Prepare clean pots with soil and then transfer the seedlings. Water scantily at first; again, this is a crucial time, and seedlings must be given somewhat more care than usual. Increase light gradually, and water more often as plants increase in size. In about a month plants can be placed in bright light and given routine waterings.

## Grafting

Grafting offers the plant hobbyist a fascinating way of seeing nature at work. It is one way to get difficult plants to root, and it also creates such plant oddities as crests and other unusual shapes not often seen in the plant world. Grafted plants usually grow more quickly than plants propagated by cuttings. Not all succulents and cacti can be grafted; the best ones are from the milkweed and Euphorbia families because plants in these groups have a cambium layer, which is essential for grafting.

The three common grafting methods are flat, cleft, and side. For first attempts, try the flat graft, which is the easiest. This involves fitting a flat base to a flat top. Fit the scion cut (the one with a flat base) to an underside cut (the one with a flat top), pressing the two flat surfaces flush together. Use rubber bands or string to hold the union in place. (If you use toothpicks for putting any grafts together, there will be a scar.) In the cleft graft, a V-shaped base is fitted into another wedge-shaped cut. The two pieces are usually tied together with a string. The side graft entails cutting both pieces on a slant and then joining them together with string until a union is formed.

Select only healthy stock for grafting; it must support the cut until it is capable of growing on its own. Also, use plump cuts from firm growing tips or new offshoots. To be successful with grafting, you must be sure that the cut surfaces fit together flush, without any air space between them. The growth layers of both parts must be in contact with each other, and the cuts themselves must be kept free of dirt or dust. If sap starts to run from the cut parts, soak them in water for a few minutes to dissolve the sap.

Grafted plants need bright but not sunny locations and should be watered sparsely the first week or so. Occasionally check to be sure the string or rubber bands are in place. The best time to graft is from May to October. This is when plants are vigorous and have enough sap flowing to ensure a perfect union.

119. *Melocactus matanzanus*
Cuba

The Turk's Cap is a uniquely shaped plant that comes from tropical areas near sea level. It prefers warmth, humidity, and, during the growing season, ample moisture at its roots. The flowers are rose pink.

120. *Rebutia fiebrigii*
Bolivia

The harmless spines on most of the Rebutias have resulted in their being extremely desirable as pot plants. This clustering species is easily grown in a rapid-draining soil, with slight shade and a winter rest.

121. *Epiphyllum crenatum*
Honduras; Guatemala

This species, known as Orchid Cactus, like most Epiphyllums, prefers some shade, light soil, and generous watering during the summer growing period. Like other epiphytic cacti, it prefers growing in a hanging basket or other suspended container. The fragrant flowers are four to eight inches across.

122. *Euphorbia aerugnosa*
North Transvaal

This is an extremely beautiful succulent among the thin-stemmed Euphorbias. The species name here refers to the blue-green color of verdigris or oxidized copper. The plant remains small, under six inches, and produces bright yellow flowers in the winter.

123. *Rhipsalis rhombea*
Brazil

This spineless cactus, which normally grows up in the trees in its natural habitat, produces an abundance of flowers each spring. Being epiphytic, it prefers a light soil mixture, ample water, and partial shade.

124. *Parodia camarguensis*
Peru

In most Parodias the interesting arrangement of ribs and spines creates attractive plants, even when they are not blooming. These cacti also tend to be small specimens which are well suited to windowsill culture. In order to produce their large flowers (two inches across in this species), a cool, dry, winter rest is required.

125. Sempervivum Hybrid

The numerous Sempervivum species of mountainous Europe and Asia have been hybridized repeatedly, and, as a result, the hundreds of existing hybrids are very difficult to identify. In fact, many of them have never been named. This particular one is especially attractive, producing a six- to eight-inch brilliantly colored rosette and many small offsets. Being winter hardy, this genus deserves more attention than it receives, particularly in the United States.

126. *Sedum sieboldii*
Japan

This winter-hardy succulent dies back to the roots each season, but is an ideal hanging-basket subject for moderately cold climates. The flowers appear in autumn, and the approach of winter turns the blue-green leaves to beautiful shades of red and soft violet.

127. *Euphorbia lactea cristata*
India; Ceylon

This twenty-inch-tall plant bears little resemblance to the normal form of *Euphorbia lactea*. A beautiful specimen of this age and size is rare. The plant requires warmth for good growth.

128. *Tavaresia grandiflora*
Southwest Africa

A member of the Starfish Flower family, this somewhat delicate plant produces enormous, exotic blossoms. It likes warmth and must be watered very cautiously during the winter rest period.

129. *Euphorbia milii splendens*
Madagascar

The familiar Crown of Thorns is a sprawling plant which produces an abundance of brilliant flowers sporadically. It is one of the easiest succulents to grow. However, it needs a good amount of sunlight in order to flower.

130. *Rebutia canigueralii*
Bolivia

The tiny Rebutias, producing flowers up to an inch in diameter, grow amid grass at high elevations, where they receive a generous amount of rainfall during the growing season. In their habitat they are somewhat shaded by the grass which surrounds them.

131. *Haworthia greenii*
Cape Province

This plant branches from the base and forms a beautiful clump eight to ten inches high. Although slow growing, it offers no particular problems in cultivation. Like most of the Haworthias, it prefers partial shade and generous watering during the growing period.

132. *Crassula falcata*
South Africa

Six- to eight-inch-long sickle-shaped leaves of a gray-green color characterize this satisfying plant. The immense, brilliant red flower heads remain in good condition for a long period of time. It is of easy cultivation, and like many Crassulas, is somewhat cool growing and likes generous watering during the growing period.

133. *Matucana calliantha*
Peru

The genus Matucana was named for the town of the same name in Peru. Additional species, since discovered in valleys below this area, are very closely related and should, perhaps, be placed in the same genus. Whatever the name, Matucana or Submatucana, this plant is a beautiful, rather uncommon, species. The one and one-half inch flowers are produced in groups of two or three.

134. *Glottiphyllum nelii*
South Africa

The tonguelike leaves of this succulent are almost hidden by the two-inch blossoms which are produced in summer. It is an unassuming plant which is easy to grow.

135. *Mammillaria schwarzii*
Mexico

This is one of the most desirable of all the Mammillarias. It is easy to grow, and the tiny clustering plants, thickly covered with harmless white hair (spines), create a perfect background for the pale yellow flowers.

136. *Echinocactus grusonii*
Central Mexico

*Mammillaria geminispina*
Mexico

The Golden Barrel Cactus seen here in the background is an easily grown plant which may reach four feet or more in diameter. The spectacular clumps of *Mammillaria geminispina* in the foreground have required many years to reach this size.

119

120

121

122

123

126

127

128

129    130

131    132

134

135

136

# Nine ✳ Greenhouse Growing

The nice thing about greenhouse growing is that you can keep plants there all year and use several at selected times to decorate the home—just the way orchids used to be grown. You can grow many plants that you could not manage in the home, and there is always sufficient light so plants will bloom.

But because cacti and succulents require more air circulation and less humidity than other plants, it is a good idea to devote a separate part of the greenhouse to them.

## Conditions and Care

Most greenhouses have more than adequate humidity, which can affect plants adversely. You must prevent a close, stagnant atmosphere; for best results, keep humidity at fifty percent and always provide excellent ventilation, even in winter. In the summer, when the sun is directly overhead, protect plants from scorching by using a lattice-panel arrangement or old-fashioned whiting.

Try to avoid any dripping water in the greenhouse because cacti and succulents can rot if water consistently drips on them. Water with a hose or watering can, but be sure to do it early in the morning so by nightfall leaves are dry. I keep my cacti and succulents in pots on slatted benches in my greenhouse because this provides air from the bottom.

Plants in the greenhouse will be subject to more insect attack than plants in homes because wherever you grow a group of plants together, the insect proliferation is apt to be greater than if you have only a few plants. Thus, keep a vigil for pests; if you see them, take immediate steps to get rid of them.

Always keep the greenhouse free of any debris and dirt. In fact, the greenhouse should be as scrupulously clean as your own kitchen—maintenance and sanitary conditions are a must in greenhouse growing.

Greenhouse culture requires somewhat more care than home growing. Plants will have adequate light all year so you must water them more regularly and make sure they have adequate nutrients. Use plant food more often for greenhouse plants, but never overdo it.

As in home growing, water plants somewhat lightly during spring and fall. But during the summer months, most species can take plenty of water. For the majority of cacti and succulents, watering should be sparse, if at all, in the winter. Soil should be kept just barely moist. And in the winter, temperatures should be cooler, from 50 to 55°F, for plants to thrive. This winter rest is essential if you want plants to bloom.

## Advantages

We have cited some advantages of growing cacti and succulents in greenhouses but perhaps the major factor is that most plants will bloom under glass. There is adequate light and moisture, and cacti and some succulents produce magnificent flowers, as described in Chapter 1. You will have a symphony of color through spring and summer.

It is important to remember that plants in bud are temperamental, and buds can drop if temperatures are too cold or too hot. However, once buds are fully formed you can move plants to the home for indoor decoration. Enjoy them while they are in flower and then return them to the greenhouse afterward.

As a rule, plants will grow quicker in a greenhouse than in the home. There will never be rapid growth but generally plants will mature and blossom quicker under glass than at windows, where light is not at its best.

If you have a greenhouse collection of plants, pay particular attention to artificial light coming from the house (if the greenhouse is a lean-to) or putting on artificial light in the greenhouse at night. Many plants are light sensitive and even a few minutes of artificial light can deter or completely hinder plants from blossoming. However, the greenhouse is rarely used at night so this should not be a major problem.

Cacti and succulents either bloom during the day or at night. Indeed, many cacti, such as several Cereus and Hylocereus, do bloom at night. The majority, however, are day bloomers. Once flowers have opened it is all right to have them in artificial light.

If you know in which season plants bloom you can arrange your greenhouse with spring bloomers at one end and summer-blossoming types in another. This way you can observe and expect bloom and also have an array of color most of the year.

# Ten ✳ Landscaping Ideas

If you have the property, landscaping with cacti and succulents is an exciting experience and a unique way to have a garden. The unusual forms and shapes, colors and flowers create an almost fairyland type of garden. If you live in regions such as Texas, Arizona, parts of California, and New Mexico, the beauty of cacti and succulents in the landscape cannot be ignored. And once plants are in the ground, they practically take care of themselves. However, some planning—including the choosing of plants—is necessary.

In my last home I had a barren south hillside facing the house. I planted many cacti and succulents, and they grew lavishly. The information in this chapter is based on the growing of these plants over a five-year period in Mill Valley, California.

## The Landscape Plan

My hillside was a tough site to work with because the terrain was difficult to climb and hard to work. On the other hand, the slope of the hill was excellent for drainage, so I decided to tackle the job. I was familiar with the handsome rosette shapes of Agaves, so I formed my garden around several types of Agaves and Aloes. I randomly placed five very large plants (about two feet across) to cover the area.

Once these plants were in place, I realized that some vertical accent was necessary, so I started looking for some large Cereus-type cacti. At that time large specimens were not as much in demand as they are now, and I was able to buy three columnar-branching cacti fairly inexpensively. I planted these cacti in a sawtooth design at the very rear of the garden, as a framework. Because the terrain was not rocky, I knew I would have to put in some rocks to create a balance and to hold the smaller plants like Chamaecereus and Echinopsis. I bought rocks at the local building yard and had them installed on the hill. (You can install rocks yourself by digging out some soil, embedding the rock, and then replacing soil around the base to achieve a natural look.)

I used many barrel-type cacti throughout the garden and supplemented them with finger-type Kleinia succulents, again to create both vertical and horizontal patterns. I also planted several Crassulas and Cotyledon plants and here and there put in an Ice Plant or members of the Mesembryanthemum family as ground covers.

The first year the garden seemed sparse, but by the second year, once plants had started into growth and had become at home, the overall look was harmonious. And once the ground cover started to spread, the cacti and succulent garden was the main attraction at my house. In the third year bloom was abundant. Only the Cotyledons did not survive. All the other plants did beautifully, even over the winters, when temperatures fell to lows of about 38 to 40°F.

1. ROCK GARDEN

2. FREEFORM FLOATING GARDEN

3. WALL PLANTINGS

4. FOUNDATION GARDEN

# CACTUS IN LANDSCAPE

# Care

Cacti and succulents do need good drainage, and outdoors these plants require more water than you would think during the summer, especially in full sun. In fall and winter reduce moisture. This will harden the plants so they can withstand lower temperatures. (Interestingly, it is not the cold alone that damages plants; it is the combination of wet soil and soft growth that makes a freeze so hazardous.)

Plant cacti and succulents in generous holes; I dug down twenty-four to thirty inches for the larger plants. I used a standard outdoor soil mix, but added sand to it. I also used a one-half-inch layer of gravel around the base of the plants. Smaller plants were planted in holes about twelve to sixteen inches. Planting was always a problem, even when wearing gloves, because some cacti have long needle-like spines. Take your time, and have sticks and stones to help prop plants to get them into the ground.

Do not water plants at first; let them adjust for about a week. (Of course if it rains, there is little you can do.) Feed only a few times a year with ten-ten-five fertilizer.

If you do not have a slope for cacti and succulents, plant them in mounds of soil. Provide adequate drainage by putting broken stones at the base of the mounds. Only in a hilly terrain do these plants look attractive, so some work with the soil is necessary. Bring in large stones, as mentioned, to create a harmonious grouping.

You can have a cacti and succulent garden even if you are in climates where winters are severe. Select a small hill or another area that is sunny. Leave plants in their pots and sink the pots to their rims in the soil. Pay attention to vertical and horizontal accents and arrange plants so you create a small attractive garden. Use large and small specimens and be sure to give plants plenty of water during the summer months if it does not rain. When temperatures drop below 55°F, move the plants back inside the home, but first carefully inspect the pots for insects and then clean the pot surfaces.

I had no insect problems outdoors; my plants were healthy, and pests migrated to other plants that were easier to eat. However, if you do encounter insects in the outdoor garden, use a general insect spray like malathion.

# Outdoor Plants

*Agave americana* (Century Plant). A six-foot rosette packed with sword-shaped leaves having sharp teeth along the margins; indestructible.

*A. angustifolia* 'Marginata.' Large rosette of spear-shaped white and green leaves.

*A. attenuata*. Big and bold, with soft, gray-green, sword-shaped leaves in rosettes to five feet across; spineless.

*A. filifera compacta*. Olive green leaves arranged in a circular rosette; curly threads at margins.

*A. macroacantha*. Gray-green stiff leaves with black spines.

*A. parryi huachucensis*. Like granite sculpture, this rosette of tightly packed leaves has black spines at the edges.

*A. schidigera* 'Taylori.' Large rosette; curly threads on leaf margins.

*A. tequilana*. Tall; rosettes of stiff, blue-green leaves.

*Aloe africana* (Spiny Aloe). Treelike aloe with long, narrow, pointed leaves; yellow to orange flowers.

*A. palmeri*. Rosette of gray-green leaves; tough and robust.

*A. plicatilis* (Fan Aloe). Branching tree to fifteen feet with rounded, tongue-shaped, closely set leaves.

*A. striata* (Coral Aloe). Spineless, gray-green leaves bordered in red.

*A. vera*. Pointed, gray-green leaves to eighteen inches long carried in rosettes on short stems; yellow flowers.

*Carnegiea gigantea* (Giant Saguaro). Treelike, with many ribs and stout branches curving upward; slow, but eventually a giant.

*Cereus hildmannianus*. Tall and columnar, branching; large white flowers.

*C. peruvianus* (Apple Cactus or Peruvian Torch). Treelike, with blue-green branches and needle spines; white flowers, six to seven inches long, bloom at night.

*Cleistocactus strausii* (Silver Torch). Erect plant covered with white spines, branching at base with erect stems; dark red flowers.

*Echinocactus grusonii* (Golden Barrel). Big (to four feet high) and round, with golden yellow spines.

*Echinocereus reichenbachii* (Lace Cactus). Spines form a lacy covering over plant.

*Euphorbia candelabrum*. Tall, columnar growth, gray-green.

*E. echinus*. Branching, upright growth, dark green with light gray spines.

*E. grandicornis* (Cow Horn Cactus). Angular contorted ribs with brown to gray spines.

*E. ingens.* Tall growing, leafless and spiny, develops into inverted cone shape.

*Ferocactus wislizenii* (Fishhook Cactus). Cylindrical plant with fierce spines; yellow flowers sometimes edged in red.

*Furcraea gigantea.* Rosette of shiny green, narrow, spiny leaves to seven feet long; similar to Agave.

*Kalanchoe beharensis* (Elephant Ears or Felt Plant). Usually unbranched, a four- to ten-foot plant with eight-inch triangular to lance-shaped leaves covered with white to tan hairs; leaf edges heavily waved and crimped.

*Lemaireocereus marginatus.* Spiny, treelike growth with white-margined stems.

*L. thurberi* (Arizona Organ Pipe Cactus). Ribbed, columnar cactus, sometimes branching from base; eventually fifteen to twenty feet tall; purplish flowers at night.

*Opuntia basilaris* (Beaver Tail Cactus). Low growing to four feet; leaves are flat, oval pads, nearly spineless.

*Pachycereus pringlei* (Elephant Cactus). Columnar, with woody trunk and ribbed branches; to twenty-five feet.

*Trichocereus chiloensis.* Columnar plant, beautiful olive green; stiff, dark gray spines.

*T. spachianus* (Torch or White Torch Cactus). Strong, short, columnar growth; branches are parallel to main stem.

*Yucca aloifolia* (Spanish Bayonet). Branching, with stiff, dark green leaves that come to sharp points; single trunk or branched, to ten feet.

*Y. brevifolia* (Joshua Tree). Slow growth to fifteen to thirty feet with heavy trunk, few branches; short, broad, sword-shaped leaves.

*Y. elephantipes (Y. gigantea).* For large gardens only; fast growing to fifteen to thirty feet with several trunks; narrow, four-foot leaves without spiny tips.

*Y. glauca.* Leaves one and one-half to two feet long, one-half inch wide, margined with white on a nearly stemless plant; summer flowers are white.

*Y. recurvifolia.* Leaves are blue-gray-green, two to three feet long, two inches wide with harmless spine at tip; six to ten feet, usually branchless, with offsets at base to form a clump.

*Y. whipplei* (Our Lord's Candle). Stemless, with dense cluster of gray-green, sharp-pointed leaves to two feet long; flowering stem six to fourteen feet tall.

# Patios and Terraces

Potted succulents and cacti are handsome on patios and terraces and almost care for themselves. You can use some of your indoor plants outside to both refresh them and decorate the area. When something different is wanted outdoors, the ball- and melon-type cacti are handsome, and a large Agave in a decorative pot is stunning. Patio plants are always on display, so choose the most distinctive types, like a large Echinocactus or a symmetrical Agave. The *very* large torch-type cactus is difficult to find, but a large Torch Cactus in an ornamental pot is a stellar sight.

The choice of container is important outdoors, so be sure plant and pot complement each other. Pay attention to scale; neither plant nor container should overbalance the other. Potted plants outdoors need a very porous soil so that water can penetrate readily and drain quickly. Use equal parts of loam and topsoil and add some sand and crushed rock to be sure soil has air spaces in it. Feed outdoor plants monthly with a ten-ten-five plant food. In summer, water plants at least once a week if there is no rain; in winter, give plants a suitable place indoors where temperatures are about 55 to 60°F. Many of your indoor plants can double as patio and terrace accents in summer and be returned to the home in September.

# Wall Gardens

The landscape arrangement of cacti and succulents is most popular, but these plants can also be grown attractively on walls. If you have a bare wall, many of the smaller Sedums, Cotyledons, and Kleinias are natural subjects. Since they grow beautifully out of pockets of stone, and many are cascading, they will drape the wall in color. For planting in cold regions, use Sedums and Sempervivums, but in frost-free areas you can grow almost any succulent or cactus. Give the plants routine care and plenty of water in hot weather, but not as much when temperatures dip.

Do trim plants occasionally to encourage branching out and fresh growth. Remove decayed stems or dead leaves and keep the garden in a sculptured design, allowing some of the wall to show as a foil for the plants.

Excellent wall-garden plants are:

Aeonium hybrids. Rosettes of bright green on trailing stems.

*Cotyledon barbeyi.* Trailing stems with small, pale green leaves; natural cascader.

*Echeveria elegans.* Silver-blue rosettes; small, good.

*Kleinia tomentosa.* Finger-like growth in masses trailing down walls. Blue-green is the color; nice accent.

Sedum. (See ground cover list in the next section of this chapter.)

Sempervivums. These crawl and creep rather than trail, but they love wall growing so use them for a splendid show.

## Ground Covers

Succulents are used frequently in mild winter climates as ground covers, and they make a beautiful carpet of color. They are almost maintenance-free and deserve attention where they can be used. (No grass mowing or tending.) Plants spread rapidly, grow in poor soil, and help to hold hills because root structure acts as a binder.

Known as Ice Plants, these succulents deserve attention first as ground covers. Most have lovely foliage—gray-green or dark green stick-type leaves and handsome flowers. (See list at end of this chapter.)

Another excellent group of plants for ground covers are Sedums; these grow like weeds once established and quickly cover an area where other plants will not grow, such as in poor soil, or where lawns are impossible to have (on slopes, for example). Sedums seem to thrive in drought or rain, in sun or shade. They are greedy plants and will become invasive, so use them with discretion.

Here is a brief rundown on some Sedums:

*Sedum acre.* Fast-spreading type with yellow flowers.

*S. rubrotinctum.* Bronze-tinted leaves.

*S. sieboldii.* Popular pink-flowered trailer.

You can also use some of the Kleinias as ground cover. These plants have fleshy stems and thistle-like flowers. Perhaps the best is *Kleinia repens* with blue-green leaves. Larger plants include *K. pendula* and *K. mandraliscae,* which are from twelve to sixteen inches tall.

## Ice Plants

These small plants have innumerable uses in landscapes and are the easiest of plants to grow. In northern climates Ice Plants are treated as annuals, but in mild winter climates they are classed as perennials. These succulent plants offer blazing color and have the ability to control erosion on hills. Their drawback is their general lack of winter hardiness, but some can certainly be used as container plants for patios or even indoors for year-round color because even the foliage is attractive and most are small plants.

Ice Plants deserve more popularity with gardeners, but unfortunately the naming of these plants has been a problem. Once listed as Mesembryanthemums, they are now sold under various names such as Cephalophyllum, Drosanthemum, Lampranthus, and Maleophora. The following list will help you select Ice Plants:

Cephalophyllum (Red Spike Ice Plant). Brilliant two-inch cerise flowers; pointed, gray-green leaves about four inches high.

Delosperma (White Trailing Ice Plant). Small white flowers and dark green foliage to about two inches long.

Drosanthemum (Rose Ice Plant). Pink to purple small flowers and tiny glistening gray-green leaves.

*Lampranthus spectabilis.* (Bush-type Ice Plant). Brilliantly colored red flowers; many varieties. Gray-green two-inch leaves.

Maleophora (Trailing Ice Plant). Fine yellow flowers; thin-type gray-green foliage. Species *M. crocea,* bearing red flowers, is also available.

# Eleven ✳ Some Collector's Plants and Rare Plants

There are so many unusual cacti and succulents that it is difficult to make a selection, but some, such as Tavaresia and Copiapoa, deserve mention for they are uncommonly beautiful. So whether you consider this chapter as rare and unusual plants or collector's items or specials, all the plants are worth having (and many of these may be difficult to find).

In addition, the group of plants known as Living Stones certainly deserve mention, for these plants (mainly for collectors) are the oddities of the plant world. For all good purposes they do look like living stones and more unique plants are hard to find.

Finally, there are some plant families that have only a few succulent members, such as Tradescantia and Peperomia; these are not well known but deserve space because they are so distinctive. Also included are a few plants from houseplant groups such as Bromeliads and Begonias.

## Uncommon Cacti and Succulents

Some plants simply capture the public fancy and are given common names such as Golden Barrel and become a part of any good plant collection. Others, either not readily available or without common names to distinguish them or simply overlooked, are worth attention too; therefore, in this listing we include some rare plants for the adventurer. These are really different plants, and sometimes you may be the only one in town with a specimen, but as time goes on more unusual species will be available.

Here is a partial list of both uncommon and uncommonly beautiful cacti and succulents:

*Anacampseros alstonii.* A succulent with leaves arranged in a spiral; leaves are oval and narrow, like short green spikes; flowers generally rose-colored on short spikes.

*Bursera microphylla.* Resembles a small bonsai tree, with branching growth; tiny leaves. Unusual succulent.

*Cephalocereus pentaedrophorus.* Columnar, light green ribbed cactus; tufts of sharp spines on margins.

*Copiapoa tenuissima.* Dark green globe cactus with woolly crown and light spines; usually yellow flowers.

*Hamatocactus hamatacanthus.* Dark green globular plant; ribbed, marginal, and central spines; flowers pale yellow with red throat.

*Matucana calliantha.* Globe-type cactus, short spines; fine red flowers. Also called *Borzicactus calliantha.*

*Monadenium guentheri.* Handsome succulent branching plant; leaflike appendages on tall columns.

*Pedilanthus tithymaloides cucullatus* (Devil's Backbone). Branching succulent plant with cylindrical stems and four-inch leathery leaves that usually fall in winter.

*Stephanocereus leucostele.* Columnar, ribbed, marginal spines. Also known as *Cereus leucostele.*

*Tavaresia grandiflora.* Bright green elongated growth with fine hairs; a beautiful succulent.

*Uebelmannia pectinifera.* Handsome ribbed cactus with an almost crinkle finish, crowned with black spines.

Weingartia species. Globular cactus, wavy and ribbed, with dark spines.

## Living Stones

No cacti and succulent book would be complete without some mention of the fascinating group called Living Stones. These plants resemble tiny pebbles and hardly seem like plants. Their masquerade is on purpose: to blend into the landscape so they are not seen by marauders. Coming from the dry areas of South Africa, the Living Stones consist of a pair of fleshy leaves that act as water reservoirs. The leaves are rounded and grow low on the ground to conserve as much moisture as possible. Sunlight reaches the plant through translucent window-like devices in the leaf tips and the plants are true mimics—their form and color can fool the best eye. Only when the plants bloom are they easily seen.

There are about twenty genera but perhaps Lithops, which contain about seventy species, is the most often grown. These plants are small and conical, one inch high, with a pair of fleshy flat top leaves separated by a cleft. *Lithops lesliei* and *L. hallii* are the most common.

In the genus Conophytum the leaves are fleshy again and joined with only a slight cleft. The plants are cone-shaped, usually gray, and sometimes marbled with color. *Conophytum marnerianum* and *C. minutum* are two suggested species.

Fenestraria species live in the desert and bury themselves in sand so that only the tops of the leaves are visible. In cultivation, where there is less light and heat, the leaves should not be buried or they may rot. *Fenestraria rhopalophylla* is the only species I have seen in this group.

Living Stones also appear in the Argyroderma and Glottiphyllum genera: *Argyroderma testiculare* and *Glottiphyllum nelii,* unusual plants to say the least, have short rounded leaves.

Grow Living Stones in equal parts of soil and pebbles (finely crushed). Use shallow containers and be sure plants have good drainage; any water at the bottom of the medium will harm the plants. During cold and cloudy weather (winter as well) do not give them any moisture. Only when they start growing should they have water

and then only small amounts. Be sure the plants get several hours of sun a day and are placed where temperatures never go below 55°F.

## Night-Blooming Cereus

These climbing cacti were popular some decades ago and have recently gained followers again. Because they are not easy to locate they must be classified as collector's plants at this time. The night-blooming types produce mammoth flowers, some seven inches across, and they are startlingly beautiful.

The best known of these climbing giants (they can grow to mammoth proportions: from seven to ten feet long) are the Hylocereus and Selenicereus plants that have vinelike, thin green stems and long aerial roots. The plants clamber and crawl to great lengths and once established in a large tub they practically take care of themselves; they do, however, need some support such as a trellis or a wood grid of some sort.

The magnificent flowers open after midnight and some perfume an entire room but, alas, by morning they are dead. However, a mature plant will bear many blooms over a period of several days.

For all their beauty the plants are easy to grow; they need even moisture all year—the soil mix should never become soggy or dry. They like sunlight and can adjust to coolness if necessary, about 50°F at night. Indeed, the cool nights will help them to produce buds.

The old-fashioned favorites are *Hylocereus undatus,* with glistening white flowers, and *Selenicereus macdonaldiae,* often called the Queen of the Night; its gold-and-white blossoms often reach a foot in diameter. Equally good are *S. grandiflorus* and *S. pteranthus.*

## Holiday Cacti

In this book I have mentioned the many holiday-blooming cacti, and these rewarding houseplants are old favorites. The Christmas plants are sometimes called Zygocactus or Schlumbergera, depending upon which book you happen to read. In either case, these are jungle cacti with dark green flattened stems; blooms range in size from one to three inches across in vivid shades of red, cerise, or magenta.

These plants grow best in equal parts of fir

bark (at suppliers) and soil and prefer small containers. Keep the potting mix moderately moist all year except in fall, when some dryness is needed to encourage flower buds. At this time, place plants in cooler (55°F) locations.

In fall, see that holiday-blooming cacti have at least twelve hours of uninterrupted darkness daily for at least four weeks. Any light that reaches the plants during the dark period can interrupt or completely hinder bud formation. Once buds appear, plants can be put in their regular places at windows and routine watering resumed.

## Succulents in Other Plant Families

In Chapter 2, I discussed many groups of succulent plants that are wholly or partly succulent, but there are some families of plants that have only a few succulent members: Commelinaceae (Wandering Jew group) contains *Tradescantia navicularis* and *T. sillamontana*, the White Velvet Plant. Common houseplants such as Begonias and Peperomias also have a few succulent cousins: namely, *Begonia venosa, Peperomia rauhii,* and *P. arifolia grandis.*

In the popular plant family Bromeliaceae there are several succulent plants including *Dyckia brevifolia* and *Abromeitiella chlorantha;* even the Coleus clan has a succulent offspring: *Coleus aromatica.*

More than two hundred and fifty different plants have been discussed in this book and there are hundreds more—in fact, enough plants to keep you busy several lifetimes. And this world of plants contains some of the most unusual and uncommonly beautiful treasures of nature one can find. These are plants that offer a continual adventure and provide years of beauty indoors and out.

## Cacti by Common Name

| | | | |
|---|---|---|---|
| Apple Cactus | *Cereus peruvianus* | Indian Head | *N. ottonis* |
| Arizona Organ Pipe Cactus | *Lemaireocereus thurberi* | Lace Cactus | *Echinocereus reichenbachii* |
| Aztec Column | *Cephalocereus polyanthus* | Lemon Ball | *Notocactus mammulosus* |
| Beaver Tail Cactus | *Opuntia basilaris* | Link Cactus | *Rhipsalis paradoxa* |
| Bishop's Cap | *Astrophytum myriostigma* | Night-Blooming Cereus | *Hylocereus undatus* |
| Blue Barrel | *Echinocereus ingens* | | *Selenicereus macdonaldiae* |
| Bunny Ears | *Opuntia microdasys* | Old Lady Cactus | *Mammillaria hahniana* |
| Chin Cactus | *Gymnocalycium mihanovichii* | Old Man Cactus | *Cephalocereus senilis* |
| Christmas Cactus | *Schlumbergera bridgesii* | Old Man Opuntia | *Opuntia vestita* |
| | *Zygocactus truncatus* | Orchid Cactus | Epiphyllums |
| Crimson Parodia | *Parodia sanguiniflora* | Organ Pipe Cactus | *Lemaireocereus thurberi* |
| Crown Cactus | *Rebutia minuscula* | Paraguay Ball | *Notocactus schumannianus* |
| Eagle Claw Cactus | *Echinocereus horizonthalonius* | Peanut Cactus | *Chamaecereus sylvestri* |
| Easter Cactus | *Schlumbergera bridgesii* | Peruvian Torch | *Cereus peruvianus* |
| Easter Lily Cactus | *Echinopsis multiplex* | Powder Puff Cactus | *Mammillaria bocasana* |
| Elephant Cactus | *Pachycereus pringlei* | Queen of the Night | *Selenicereus macdonaldiae* |
| Fire Crown | *Rebutia senilis* | | |
| Fishhook Cactus | *Ferocactus wislizenii* | Rainbow Cactus | *Echinocereus dasyacanthus* |
| | *Mammillaria microcarpa* | | *E. rigidissimus* |
| Giant Saguaro | *Carnegiea gigantea* | Rattail Cactus | *Aporocactus flagelliformis* |
| Goat's Horn Cactus | *Astrophytum capricorne* | Red Crown | *Rebutia minuscula* |
| Golden Ball | *Notocactus leninghausii* | Rice Cactus | *Rhipsalis cereuscula* |

| | |
|---|---|
| Scarlet Ball | *Notocactus haselbergii* |
| Scarlet Bugler Cactus | *Cleistocactus baumannii* |
| Shining Ball | *Echinopsis calochlora* |
| Silver Ball | *Notocactus scopa* |
| Silver Torch | *Cleistocactus strausii* |
| Snowball Cactus | *Mammillaria bocasana* |
| Star Cactus | *Astrophytum ornatum* |
| Teddy Bear Cactus | *Opuntia bigelovii* |
| Tom Thumb Cactus | *Parodia aureispina* |
| Torch Cactus | *Trichocereus spachianus* |
| Totem Pole | *Lophocereus schottii* |
| Turk's Cap | *Melocactus matanzanus* |
| Whisker Cactus | *Lophocereus schottii 'Monstrosus'* |
| White Chin Cactus | *Gymnocalycium schickendantzii* |
| White Torch Cactus | *Trichocereus spachianus* |
| Woolly Torch Cactus | *Cephalocereus palmeri* |

## Succulents by Common Name

| | |
|---|---|
| Baby Toes | *Fenestraria rhopalophylla* |
| Baked Beans | *Sedum stahlii* |
| Basketball Plant | *Euphorbia obesa* |
| Burro's Tail | *Sedum morganianum* |
| Calico Hearts | *Adromischus maculatus* |
| Century Plant | *Agave americana* |
| Chalk Lettuce | *Dudleya brittonii* |
| Chalk Plant | *Kleinia tomentosa* |
| Chenille Plant | Echeveria |
| Christmas Poinsettia | *Euphorbia pulcherrima* |
| Coral Aloe | *Aloe striata* |
| Cow Horn Cactus | *Euphorbia grandicornis* |
| Crown of Thorns | *E. milii splendens* |
| Elephant Bush | *Portulacaria afra* |
| Elephant Ears | *Kalanchoe beharensis* |
| Fan Aloe | *Aloe plicatilis* |
| Felt Plant | *Kalanchoe beharensis* |
| Ghost Plant | *Graptopetalum paraguayense* |
| Golden Sedum | *Sedum adolphi* |
| Golden-Spined Aloe | *Aloe nobilis* |
| Hen and Chicks | Sempervivums |
| Houseleeks | Sempervivums |
| Ice Plants | Delosperma Drosanthemum Lampranthus Maleophora |

| | |
|---|---|
| Inchworm Plant | *Kleinia pendula* |
| Jade Plant | *Crassula argentea* |
| Joshua Tree | *Yucca brevifolia* |
| Lace Aloe | *Aloe aristata* |
| Leopard Spots | *Adromischus maculatus* |
| Little Pickles | *Othonna capensis* |
| Living Stones | *Argyroderma testiculare* *Ariocarpus trigonus* *Conophytum marnerianum* *C. minutum* *Fenestraria rhopalophylla* *Glottiphyllum nelii* *Lithops lesliei* *L. hallii* |
| Midget Pink | *Crassula tetragona* |
| Moonstones | *Pachyphytum oviferum* |
| Our Lord's Candle | *Yucca whipplei* |
| Ox Tongue | *Gasteria verrucosa* |
| Painted Lady | *Echeveria derenbergii* |
| Panda Plant | *Kalanchoe tomentosa* |
| Partridge Breast Aloe | *Aloe variegata* |
| Pea Plant | *Senecio rowleyanus* |
| Plover's Eggs | *Adromischus cooperi* |
| Plush Plant | *Echeveria pulvinata* |
| Poinsettia | *Euphorbia pulcherrima* |
| Pony Tail Plant | *Beaucarnea recurvata* |
| Sea Onion | *Bowiea volubilis* |
| Silver Beads | *Crassula deltoidea* |
| Silver Dollar | *C. arborescens* |
| Spanish Bayonet | *Yucca aloifolia* |
| Spiny Aloe | *Aloe africana* |
| Spiral Aloe | *A. polyphylla* |
| Starfish Flowers | Stapelias |
| String of Buttons | *Crassula perforata* |
| String of Hearts | *Ceropegia woodii* |
| Thread Plant | *Agave filifera* |
| Tiger Aloe | *Aloe variegata* |
| Tiger's Jaws | *Faucaria tigrina* |
| Wandering Jew | *Tradescantia navicularis* |
| Wax Plant | *Hoya carnosa* |
| White Velvet Plant | *Tradescantia sillamontana* |
| Zebra Haworthia | *Haworthia fasciata* |

## Most Popular Cacti

*Astrophytum myriostigma*
*Cephalocereus senilis*
*Cereus peruvianus*

*Chamaecereus sylvestri*
*Cleistocactus baumannii*
*C. strausii*
*Echinocactus grusonii*
*Echinocereus reichenbachii*
*E. rigidissimus*
*Echinopsis calochlora*
Epiphyllums
Gymnocalyciums
*Lobivia aurea*
*L. backebergii*
*Mammillaria compressa*
*M. hahniana*
*Notocactus leninghausii*
*N. ottonis*
*N. scopa*
*Opuntia microdasys*
*Parodia aureispina*
*P. sanguiniflora*
*Rebutia kupperana*
*R. minuscula*
*Rhipsalis paradoxa*
Schlumbergeras
Zygocacti

## Most Popular Succulents

*Adromischus clavifolius*
*Aeonium atropurpureum*
*Agave americana marginata*
*A. parryi huachucensis*
*A. victoriae-reginae*
*Aloe arborescens*
*A. nobilis*
*A. variegata*
*Beaucarnea recurvata*
*Ceropegia woodii*
*Cotyledon undulata*
*Crassula arborescens*
*C. argentea*
*C. deltoidea*
*Dudleya pulverulenta*
Echeveria hybrids
*Euphorbia milii splendens*
*E. obesa*
*E. pulcherrima*
*Gasteria verrucosa*
*Haworthia fasciata*

*H. tessellata*
*Hoya carnosa*
*Kalanchoe blossfeldiana*
*K. tomentosa*
*Kleinia articulata*
Sansevierias
*Sedum guatemalense*
*S. multiceps*
*S. sieboldii*
Sempervivums
Stapelias

## Flowering Times of Cacti

| *Genus* | *Season of Bloom* |
| --- | --- |
| Aporocactus | Spring |
| Ariocarpus | Summer |
| Astrophytum | Spring/Summer |
| Cephalocereus | Summer |
| Cereus | Summer/Fall |
| Chamaecereus | Summer |
| Cleistocactus | Spring/Summer/Fall |
| Coryphantha | Summer/Fall |
| Echinocactus | Summer |
| Echinocereus | Spring/Summer |
| Echinopsis | Summer/Fall |
| Ferocactus | Summer |
| Gymnocalycium | Spring/Summer/Fall |
| Hamatocactus | Summer/Fall |
| Lobivia | Summer |
| Lophophora | Spring/Summer |
| Mammillaria | Spring/Summer/Fall |
| Melocactus | Spring/Summer |
| Notocactus | Summer |
| Opuntia | Spring/Summer |
| Parodia | Spring/Summer |
| Rebutia | Spring/Summer |
| Rhipsalidopsis | Spring |
| Rhipsalis | Fall/Winter |
| Schlumbergera | Winter |
| Selenicereus | Summer |
| Strombocactus | Spring/Summer |
| Thelocactus | Summer |
| Weingartia | Summer |
| Wilcoxia | Spring/Summer |
| Zygocactus | Fall/Winter |

137. *Rhipsalis rhombea*
Brazil

A spineless and epiphytic cactus, this succulent grows in the trees in areas of moderately high rainfall. With lower temperatures and less moisture the leaves assume a beautiful red color. The small cream-colored flowers appear in early spring.

138. *Agave parryi huachucensis*
Southern Arizona; Northern Mexico

This spectacular rosette of gray-blue leaves, accented with dark red-brown spines, is a very tolerant plant. This two-foot specimen is growing in the cool, moist climate of a San Francisco garden. It forms offsets profusely, and small specimens are admirable, slow-growing pot plants.

139. *Rhipsalis cereuscula*
Uruguay; Brazil

This epiphytic cactus is an ideal hanging-basket plant for a greenhouse. Having no spines, it bears little resemblance to the popular conception of a cactus. The flowers are pink to white.

140. *Senecio haworthii, Senecio mandraliscae, Senecio kleiniaeformis*
South Africa

An incredibly beautiful combination of blue and white is displayed by this bowl planting of three Senecio species. The heavily felted, pure white leaves, approximately one and one-half inches long, are characteristic of *Senecio haworthii* on the left. It is a choice but slow-growing plant which must be kept dry during the winter rest period. The two Senecio species on the right both possess bright blue leaves of a hue which is unique in the plant world. *Senecio mandraliscae* is a vigorous and rapid-growing plant which is an admirable ground cover in California and other subtropical climates.

141. *Kalanchoe tomentosa*
Madagascar

This shrublike plant is one of the most popular succulents for windowsill and greenhouse culture. The specimen in this photograph is about six inches tall, but it may eventually grow to twenty inches. The entire plant is covered with a dense, white, hairy felt, and the leaves are tipped in dark brown. This species is very tolerant of less than ideal conditions and tends to be rapid growing. Plentiful light and pinching of the growing tips will aid in producing a compact specimen.

142. *Mammillaria elongata*
Mexico

Golden Stars is a splendid, vigorous, and rapid-growing cactus which quickly forms a dense clump of two-inch-diameter plants. The interlocking, radial spines are yellow, and the flowers are a pale straw color. It is a sensible and gratifying choice for a beginning collection. Like most cacti, it requires a cool and dry winter rest.

143. *Hamatocactus hamatacanthus*
Southern Texas; Mexico

This gratifying, easily grown plant blooms when very young, and the large yellow flowers with red throats may entirely hide the plant itself. This cactus eventually assumes a cylindrical shape, to two feet in height.

144. *Sansevieria trifasciata* 'Golden Hahnii'

This mutation of the common Mother-in-Law's Tongue or Snake Plant forms a beautiful low-growing rosette of green mottled leaves edged in brilliant yellow. Offsets around the mother plant eventually form a beautiful colony. Extremely tolerant plants which come from tropical Africa and India, the Sansevierias prefer warm shade and ample water.

145. *Agave macroacantha*
Mexico

This plant possesses enormous spines which are a beautiful shiny black color. The stiff leaves are a pleasing, soft blue-green, and the rosettes remain under eighteen inches in diameter. It is a very satisfying pot plant and produces a good number of offsets.

146. *Mammillaria conspicua*
Mexico

An extremely complex arrangement of one long central spine, tipped in black, surrounded by sixteen to twenty-five white radial spines, makes a very interesting pattern in this cactus. It grows to five or six inches tall, with rose flowers. It is an easily grown plant.

147. *Gymnocalycium saglione*
Argentina

Of all the Gymnocalyciums, the fascinating sculptural design seen here makes this one of the most desirable succulents. It may reach a foot in diameter with age, and the blossoms are a very pale pink.

148. *Notocactus magnificus*
Brazil

This recent addition to cactus collections was discovered in 1964 and has rapidly become a very popular plant. As in this specimen, it sometimes branches from the base to form a magnificent clump. The yellow flowers are two inches across.

149. Echinopsis 'Haku-Jo'

This recent Japanese hybrid is descended from the South American Echinopsis species which are such popular plants around the world. As seen in the photograph, it produces a great quantity of offsets and quickly forms a clump. This quite young specimen is approximately four inches tall. As the plant matures a heavy layer of wool covers the edges of the ten ribs.

150. *Chamaecereus sylvestri*
Argentina

The charming little Peanut Cactus produces a clump of finger-size green branches and scarlet flowers which appear in the spring. It is very easy to grow and is a good cactus for novices. However, it must have abundant light and a cool winter rest in order to produce its typical compact growth and its large blossoms. If the plant is kept dry in the winter it will survive rather low temperatures such as those which might occur in an unheated greenhouse or on a sun porch.

151. *Ferocactus histrix*
Southwestern United States; Mexico

One of the most attractive Barrel Cacti, these two-foot-wide specimens are slow growing and are tolerant of several degrees of frost. All of the Ferocactus genus must have full sun for proper development and good color.

152. *Mammillaria celsiana*
Southern Mexico

This Mammillaria presents an interesting arrangement of white radial spines and yellow central spines on each tubercle. With age the plant produces offsets to form a beautiful cluster. The small flowers are carmine.

153. *Mammillaria compressa*
Mexico

Extremely long white spines and a dark green body create a very exciting visual effect in this vigorous, fast-growing Mammillaria. It produces an enormous number of offsets and forms large clumps. The flowers are pink.

154. *Echinocactus grusonii*
Central Mexico

The Golden Barrel is one of the most spectacular and popular cacti. The yellow spines present a very interesting arrangement when observed closely.

155. *Tradescantia sillamontana*
Mexico

The White Velvet Plant is one of several succulents in the Wandering Jew group. The heavily felted foliage produces pretty lavender flowers in the summer. The entire plant dies back to ground level during the dry resting period of winter.

156. *Pedilanthus tithymaloides cucullatus*
West Indies

Sometimes called Devil's Backbone or Redbird Cactus, this plant loses most of its beautifully variegated green, pink, and cream-colored leaves during its resting period in the winter. However, the zigzag lines of the stems still make it a most interesting specimen. Culture is the same as for other members of the Euphorbia family. The small flowers are brilliant red.

157. *Yucca elata*
Texas; New Mexico; Arizona

This beautiful plant, photographed along a highway near El Paso, is a common sight in the higher grassland areas of the Southwest. Its elegant leaves, with threadlike margins, are clustered in a remarkable head atop a trunk which may reach ten feet in height. Like many of the Yuccas, some of which are called Soapweed, the roots of this plant produce a foamy detergent-like material which the American Indians may have used for cleaning purposes.

158. *Pachypodium densiflorum*
Madagascar

This spiny plant forms a thick trunk with many branches which are crowned with large, tropical-looking leaves. The conspicuous flowers appear at the beginning of the growing season. The specimen photographed here is approximately two feet tall.

159. Weingartia species
Peru

The Weingartias are closely related to the Gymnocalyciums and require somewhat the same culture. They come from high altitudes and tend to be hardy if not kept too wet. This species is about six inches tall.

160. *Cephalocereus pentaedrophorus*
Brazil

The startling effect of this slender, blue-stemmed cactus with yellow spines makes it a very desirable species. It is native to the tropical, brushy areas of Brazil, which implies that it is frost tender and likes warmth. The plant is usually unbranched and grows to approximately fifteen feet high.

161. *Stephanocereus leucostele*
Brazil

This admirable columnar plant grows to about ten feet and produces nocturnal, white flowers. It is vigorous growing and requires full sun for normal development.

162. *Trichocereus chiloensis*
Chile

This columnar plant becomes a branched tree in time, growing to twenty or twenty-five feet high. The body is a beautiful olive green color with extremely stiff, dark gray spines placed on sculptured tubercles. The flowers are white and red outside.

163. *Opuntia microdasys*
Mexico

The Bunny Ears is a very popular and easily grown small plant which is available in two well-known varieties. One type possesses white tufts and the other has golden yellow tufts.

164. *Echinopsis multiplex*
Brazil

The Easter Lily Cactus produces pale pink, eight-inch-long, trumpet-shaped flowers in the spring. The dark green plants grow to six inches in height and are deeply ribbed and studded with fierce spines. It is a vigorous and beautiful plant and has gone on record as being hardy even in the milder areas of Canada. This planting in a dark brown unglazed Japanese bowl was achieved by removing six offsets from a larger plant. They have been growing here for three years. A solitary plant will form a complete ring of offsets at its base.

165. *Mammillaria roseocentra*
Coahuila, Mexico

Spines of two different colors, white and rose red, make this a most attractive species. It offsets readily to form beautiful clumps, with individual plants being two to three inches in diameter. It produces flowers reluctantly and is somewhat uncommon in the trade.

166. *Nyctocereus serpentinus*
Mexico

In the Cereus tribe there are several species of cacti which are commonly known as night-blooming cereus. This one, sometimes referred to as 'Queen of the Night,' produces large, pure white flowers five and one-half inches in diameter on eight-inch funnels. The extremely fragrant blossoms open at dusk and close at dawn, remaining open only one night. The plants consist of slender, erect green columns which eventually tend to clamber if unsupported. This species is very desirable because it blooms prolifically while still small; the specimen seen here is a single column less than three feet tall.

Many of the well-known night-blooming cereus, such as *Hylocereus undatus* and *Selenicereus grandiflorus,* become enormous, sprawling plants and require tremendous space in a greenhouse. However, they also produce spectacular large blossoms which are even more impressive, perhaps, than *Nyctocereus serpentinus*. In Hawaii, *Hylocereus undatus* is an extremely common plant which tends to colonize along fences, creating an incredible display when it blooms in spring or early summer.

### 167. Greenhouse Cactus Collection

These well-labeled plants are resting on beds of gravel and are sprayed with an insecticide at regular intervals in order to combat scale and mealybugs.

### 168. Greenhouse Collection of Cacti

This fiber-glass structure is attached to a residence and receives a small amount of winter heat from that source. These perfectly groomed, healthy plants are jewel-like in their beauty, especially when in bloom. With the large number of species growing here, blossoms occur from late February through August.

### 169. Greenhouse Collection of Cacti

This neat arrangement of plants is a dependable entice-ment for the person who wanders into an attractive greenhouse sales area such as the one shown here. The owner carefully inspects the plants periodically in order to thwart the invasion of mealybugs and scale.

### 170. Wall Planting of Succulents

A collection of Sedums, Dudleyas, Sempervivums, Aloes, and *Senecio mandraliscae* (top right) thrives in this plant-ing which simulates the cliff sides and the steep slopes where they grow naturally. For cold climates there is a vast number of hardy cacti, Sedums, and Sempervivums which would find this rock wall perfect for their requirement of good drainage.

### 171. Succulent Collection Under Fluorescent Lights

Haworthias are an ideal choice for growing under fluores-cent lights as their needs, in terms of light, are much less than most other succulents. The foot-wide rosette of rigid, hairy leaves on the left is the succulent *Chirita sinensis,* an African Violet relative, and has been growing in this loca-tion for three years. This specimen was grown from a single leaf cutting. *Begonia venosa* (rear, right center) is another succulent suitable for lower levels of light. This basement collection is provided with an automatic timer which turns the lights on at six in the morning and off at eight in the evening. The fixture contains one cool white tube and one Gro-Lux Wide Spectrum.

### 172. Window Collection of Cacti and Other Succulents

A wide variety of plants grow happily here in a corner arrangement of two windows facing northeast and south-east. A skylight in the room provides a small amount of additional overhead light. The cooler "micro climate" in the corner of this room provides the lower winter temperatures which are ideal for all of the cacti and succulents shown here. During this resting period only enough water is given to prevent shriveling. Hardier plants are also growing on a ledge outside the window.

### 173. *Gymnocalycium andreae* X *G. baldianum*

The deep red blossom of *Gymnocalycium baldianum* ap-pears in this vigorous hybrid. The plant is about three inches in diameter, being somewhat larger than *Gym-nocalycium andreae,* which has a yellow blossom. Ease of cultivation is one of the great assets of this genus.

### 174. *Mammillaria fera-rubra*
   Mexico

The spines of this cactus, ranging in color from tan to orange-brown, are a beautiful complement to the brilliant red flowers. The plant grows to four or six inches in height, and it produces offsets.

### 175. *Stapelia youngii*
   Rhodesia

All of the Stapelia genus require a great deal of warmth, especially during the summer growth period. The five-inch starfish flowers of this species appear in mid-summer.

### 176. *Echinocereus pectinatus rigidissimus*
   Southeastern Arizona; Northern Sonora

The Arizona Rainbow Cactus is a great favorite because of its colored spines arranged in bands of white, brown, pink, and red. In cultivation, intense sunlight is necessary in order to maintain this coloration. The flowers are almost three inches long and three inches wide.

### 177. *Huernia primulina*
   Cape Province

Like the Stapelias, this related plant requires summer warmth for proper growth. The purple-throated, two-inch flowers are produced in autumn and winter.

### 178. *Conophytum marnerianum*
   Cape Province

This tiny plant, only one inch tall, requires a quickly drain-ing soil and cautious watering in the winter in order to grow properly. In time it will produce a clump such as this. The flowers are a coppery color.

### 179. *Aeonium arboreum variegata*
   Canary Islands

This beautifully variegated mutation is somewhat less vig-orous than the plain green variety. However, it is well worth the extra care required in cultivation, for the large rosettes of leaves, five to seven inches in diameter, are spectacular. It is native to a Mediterranean climate and prefers warm, somewhat dry summers and cool, rainy, frost-free winters. For best appearance it also requires par-tial shade.

### 180. *Parodia bueneckeri*
   Argentina; Bolivia

This free-flowering Parodia is one which offsets prolifically and forms large clumps. The spiral arrangement of the ribs is typical of many species in this genus. A cold winter rest is essential for this high-altitude plant.

### 181. *Gymnocalycium camarpense*
   Argentina

The majority of the Gymnocalyciums come from the east-ern slope of the Andes in Argentina, Paraguay, and Bolivia. Most of them are rather undemanding in culture and will grow well with less light than many other cacti. This par-ticular one is unique in its flower color.

### 182. *Copiapoa tenuissima*
   Northern Chile

This unique, small cactus is a very dark, almost black, shade of green, and its light-colored spines and yellow flow-ers create a startling contrast. It is somewhat slow growing, but its beauty makes it a very desirable species. The blos-soms are about one and one-half inches in diameter.

183. *Crassula argentea (portulacea)* 'Crosby's Compact'

There are many cultivars of the common Jade Plant, and this is one of the best. It is smaller growing than the common variety that is usually seen, and the leaves assume brilliant coloration with intense sun and some dryness.

184. Lobiviopsis 'Stars and Stripes'
    South America

Each spring this rather ordinary-looking cactus puts out an amazing display of three-inch-wide flowers. This plant is one of many hybrids between Lobivia and Echinopsis, both genera from the high altitudes of the Andes. Its culture is very simple: summer growth and winter rest.

185. *Mamillopsis senilis*
    Mexico

This beautiful cactus comes from the Sierra Madre of western Mexico, where it grows in forested areas at eight- to ten-thousand-foot elevations. It is trouble-free in cultivation as long as it is given a well-drained soil and a cool winter rest. The flowers are almost two inches in diameter.

186. *Parodia microthele*
    Argentina; Bolivia

The spirally arranged ribs of this cactus create a very decorative specimen, even when it is not flowering. It tends to grow as a solitary plant, which causes it to be in somewhat short supply. Propagation is by seeds.

187. *Coleus aromatica*
    Madagascar

Several succulent members of the Coleus genus have been brought into cultivation recently, and this is perhaps the most attractive one. The thick leaves have a very pungent odor, and the plant forms a compact little shrub in bright light. It likes summer warmth and generous watering during that period.

188. *Crassula erosula* 'Campfire'
    South Africa

The variety 'Campfire' assumes brilliant coloration if not overwatered or overfed. One application of fertilizer with a high percentage of nitrogen can cause the plant to turn green in a matter of days. Almost all cacti and succulents become sturdier plants, with better coloration, if given a fertilizer with a percentage of phosphorus which is higher than that of nitrogen.

137

138

140

141

142

143

144

134

146

147

148

149

150

151

152

153

154  155

156

158

159

160

161

162

163

164

165

167

169

170

171

173

174

175

176

178    179

180

181

182     183

184

185

187

188

# Where to Buy Plants

Abbey Brook Cactus Nursery
Rock House, 42 Greenhill Main Road
Sheffield, England S8 7RD

Abbey Garden
176 Toro Canyon Road
Carpinteria, California 93013

Ben Haines (cold climate cacti and succulents)
1902 Lane
Topeka, Kansas 66604

Cactus Gem Nursery
10092 Mann Drive
Cupertino, California 95014

California Epi Center (Epiphyllums)
Box 2474
Van Nuys, California 91404

Easterbrook Greenhouses (Gesneriads, Begonias)
10 Craig Street
Butler, Ohio 44822

Ed Storms (Lithops and other succulents)
4223 Pershing
Fort Worth, Texas 76107

Grigsby Cactus Gardens
2326–2354 Bella Vista
Vista, California 92083

Hahn's Cactus Nursery (no catalogue; no shipping)
2663 Loomis Drive
San Jose, California 95121

Henrietta's Nursery
1345 N. Brawley Avenue
Fresno, California 93705

Hollow Hills Succulent Farm
Route 2, Box 883
Carmel, California 93921

International Succulent Institute, Inc.
(a nonprofit organization with an annual list of rare
    cacti and other succulents)
J.W. Dodson, Secretary
10 Corte Sombrita
Orinda, California 94563

K and L Cactus Nursery
12712 Stockton Boulevard
Galt, California 95632

Kartuz Greenhouses (Begonias, Gesneriads, succu-
    lents)
92 Chestnut Street
Wilmington, Massachusetts 01887

Lauray of Salisbury (Gesneriads, Begonias, cacti,
    and succulents)
Undermountain Road (Route 41)
Salisbury, Connecticut 06068

Lila's Nursery (succulents; no cacti; no catalogue; no
    shipping)
4 Altena Street
San Rafael, California 94901

Logee's Greenhouses (Begonias, succulents, rare plants)
55 North Street
Danielson, Connecticut 06239

Mac Pherson Gardens (Sempervivums)
2920 Starr Avenue
Oregon, Ohio 43616

Modlin's Cactus Gardens
2416 El Corto
Vista, California 92083

Northside Cacti and Succulent Nursery (no catalogue; no shipping)
3658 N. 1st Street
San Jose, California 95131

Oakhill Gardens (Sedums, Sempervivums)
Route 1, Box 87F
Dallas, Oregon 97338

The Potting Shed (no phone; no catalogue; no shipping)
U.S. Route 15N.
Gordonsville, Virginia 22942

Singers' Growing Things
6385 Enfield Avenue
Reseda, California 91335

Southern Gardens
P.O. Box 547
Riverview, Florida 33569

Tanque Verde Greenhouses (no catalogue; no shipping)
10810 Tanque Verde Road
Tucson, Arizona 85715

# Bibliography

Benson, Lyman. *The Cacti of Arizona.* Tucson: University of Arizona Press, 1950.

Breitung, August. *The Agaves.* Reseda, Calif.: Abbey Garden Press, 1968.

Britton, Nathaniel, and Rose, Joseph. *The Cactaceae.* 4 vols. 1937. Reprint. New York: Dover Publications, 1963.

Brooklyn Botanic Garden. *Handbook on Succulent Plants.* Brooklyn, N.Y.: Brooklyn Botanic Garden, 1972.

*Cactus and Succulent Journal.* Vols. 38–48 (1965–1976). Reseda, Calif: Abbey Garden Press, 1976.

Carruthers, L., and Ginns, R. *Echeverias.* New York: Arco Publishing Co., 1973.

Chidamian, Claude. *The Book of Cacti and Other Succulents.* Garden City, N.Y.: Doubleday and Co., 1958.

Craig, Robert T. *The Mammillaria Handbook.* Pasadena, Calif.: Abbey Garden Press, 1945.

Gentry, Howard. *The Agave Family in Sonora.* Agriculture Handbook, no. 399. Washington, D.C.: Agricultural Research Service, 1972.

Glass, Charles, and Foster, Robert. *Cacti and Succulents for the Amateur.* New York: Van Nostrand, Reinhold Co., 1976.

Graf, Alfred. *Exotica Three.* Rutherford, N.J.: Roehrs Co., 1973.

Haage, Walther. *Cacti and Succulents.* New York: E.P. Dutton and Co., 1970.

Haselton, Scott. *Succulents for the Amateur.* Pasadena, Calif.: Abbey Garden Press, 1955.

Herre, H. *The Genera of the Mesembryanthemaceae.* Cape Town: Tafelberg-Uitgewers Beperk, 1971.

Jacobsen, Hermann. *A Handbook of Succulent Plants.* 3 vols. London: Blandford Press, 1960.

———. *Lexicon of Succulent Plants.* London: Blandford Press, 1974.

Jeppe, Barbara. *South African Aloes.* Cape Town and London: Purnell, 1969.

Kramer, Jack. *Succulents and Cactus.* Menlo Park, Calif.: Lane Books, 1970.

Lamb, Edgar. *The Illustrated Reference on Cacti and Other Succulents.* 4 vols. London: Blandford Press, 1955.

Marsden, Cyril. *Cacticulture Series.* London: Cleaver-Hume Press. Book 1, *Grow Cacti,* 1955; Book 2, *Mammillaria,* 1957.

Martin, Margaret; Chapman, P.R.; Auger, H.A. *Cacti and Their Cultivation.* New York: Winchester Press, 1971.

Reynolds, Gilbert, *The Aloes of South Africa.* Johannesburg: The Trustees, Aloes of South Africa Book Fund, 1950.

———. *The Aloes of Tropical Africa and Madagascar.* Mbabane, Swaziland: The Trustees, Aloes Book Fund, 1966.

Walther, Eric. *Echeveria.* San Francisco: California Academy of Sciences, 1972.

White, Alain, and Sloane, Boyd. *The Stapelieae.* 3 vols. Pasadena, Calif.: Abbey Garden Press, 1937.

Membership in the Cactus and Succulent Society of America is recommended. Annual dues of $12.50 include a subscription to the *Cactus and Succulent Journal,* published bimonthly. The address is: Cactus and Succulent Society of America, Inc., Box 167, Reseda, California 91335.

A large selection of books dealing with cacti and succulents may be obtained from Abbey Garden Press, Box 3010, Santa Barbara, California 93105. An annual book catalogue is published by them, containing books from many different publishers.

# Index

# Acknowledgments

My appreciation is expressed to the following individuals, cactus and succulent nurseries, dealers and public gardens for permission to photograph their collections of cacti and succulents: Antonelli Brothers, Santa Cruz, California; Botanical Gardens of the Huntington Library and Art Gallery, San Marino, California; Cactus Gem Nursery, Cupertino, California; Desert Botanical Garden, Phoenix, Arizona; Mr. J.W. Dodson, Orinda, California; Mr. Dudley B. Gold, Cuernavaca, Mexico; Hahn's Cactus Nursery, San Jose, California; International Succulent Institute, Inc., Orinda, California; Mr. and Mrs. George Jura, Berkeley, California; Mr. and Mrs. James Leaver, Lafayette, California; Lila's Nursery, San Rafael, California; Los Angeles State and County Arboretum, Arcadia, California; Moir's Plantation Gardens, Koloa, Kauai, Hawaii; Oceanside Cactus and Succulents, Capitola, California; Mr. Bartley Schwarz, Berkeley, California; Mr. and Mrs. Henry Spahn, San Diego, California; Strybing Arboretum, San Francisco, California; University of California Botanical Garden, Berkeley, California; University of California Botanical Garden, Los Angeles, California; University of Mexico Botanical Garden, Mexico City.

Don Worth
Mill Valley, California